THE VANISHING CHURCH

THE VANISHING CHURCH

How the Hollowing Out of Moderate Congregations Is Hurting Democracy, Faith, and Us

RYAN P. BURGE

BrazosPress
a division of Baker Publishing Group
Grand Rapids, Michigan

Published by Brazos Press
a division of Baker Publishing Group
Grand Rapids, Michigan
BrazosPress.com

Printed in the United States of America

Library of Congress Cataloging-in-Publication Data
Names: Burge, Ryan P. author
Title: The vanishing church : how the hollowing out of moderate congregations is hurting democracy, faith, and us / Ryan P. Burge.
Description: Grand Rapids, Michigan : Brazos Press, a division of Baker Publishing Group, [2026] | Includes bibliographical references.
Identifiers: LCCN 2025023914 | ISBN 9781587436697 cloth | ISBN 9781493453672 ebook
Subjects: LCSH: Religion—Demographic aspects—United States | United States—Religious life and customs | United States—Religion
Classification: LCC BL2525 .B874 2026
LC record available at https://lccn.loc.gov/2025023914

Cover design by Darren Welch Design

Baker Publishing Group publications use paper produced from sustainable forestry practices and postconsumer waste whenever possible.

26 27 28 29 30 31 32 7 6 5 4 3 2 1

To the faithful few of First Baptist Church
of Mount Vernon, Illinois.
Thank you for believing in me.

And to our little dog Lucy,
who was right by my side
as I wrote the first words of this book
but couldn't see it through to the end.

Contents

PART 3 A WAY FORWARD

1

No Place for Doubters

The Current State of American Religion

THE BIG TAKEAWAYS

- Moderate religion has declined rapidly—leaving a polarized religious landscape.
- Lots of people want to be part of a church, but they just can't find one where they feel comfortable.

Nine. There were nine people in the room, including myself.

As I sat facing the congregation and heard the pianist begin the service with a short prelude, I counted again. I didn't want anyone else to know what I was doing, so I tried to bounce my eyes quickly around the room. A pastor counting heads on a Sunday morning is never a good look. Thankfully, it doesn't take long to count to nine. After I was satisfied that I hadn't missed anyone hiding in the corners, the realization washed over me: We didn't break double digits that Sunday.

I knew the day was coming. Just a few years earlier, thirty of the faithful members of First Baptist Church of Mount Vernon, Illinois, would gather in this small room each Sunday to sing hymns, hear me muddle my way through a sermon, and recite the Lord's Prayer and the Apostles' Creed together. But most importantly, they were still able to continue worshiping in the same building where many of them had seen their children baptized or said final goodbyes to spouses. The vast majority had gone through every life stage in that building on the north side of town. It was the one permanent thing in their lives.

Now it was too easy to find a seat on a Sunday morning. Parking wasn't a problem at all, which was a good thing considering many members were having a hard time walking more than a hundred feet without a break. Most hymnals had gone unused for years and were gathering dust in two large stacks in the corner. In 2006, when I first began the pastorate at First Baptist, I had two of the deacons come forward and light candles, then help me serve the elements. Now, it only took about ninety seconds for me to make sure everyone was served the body and the blood.

At some point over the last seventeen years, my approach to ministry had shifted from "Let's try to revitalize this church" to "Let's make it through this Sunday." I used to think that if I preached really well and we served the community generously, our congregation would increase in size. My youthful optimism was not rewarded with numerical success. The result was that my American Baptist church, which had first been established in 1868 and was formerly one of the most prestigious congregations in town, had been reduced to a dozen retirees.

When I first took over leadership at First Baptist Church, my thoughts were almost always on the spiritual. How could I most effectively convey the hope and redemption we have through a relationship with Jesus Christ? How could our small congregation build the kingdom of God in Mount Vernon and around the world? How could I be an instrument of God's grace to those whom I had been entrusted to lead?

But over time my inner monologue had slowly begun to shift. Now the questions I was asking myself were incredibly practical. How can we sell this sixteen-thousand-square-foot building? How long can we live off the endowment? Who will take over the Brown Bag Friday program when we can't do it anymore? And all those questions were just distractions, helping me avoid the biggest and most haunting question that I was facing.

Where would I worship when my church closed its doors? Or maybe more troublesome, *Would I ever go back to church again?*

It's not something that I've ever had to worry about in life. I grew up in a conservative Southern Baptist home where church was all-encompassing. I went to church camp every summer, signed up for every mission trip, and helped organize dozens of lock-ins when I was a teenager. Right after high school I went to a Christian college that required regular chapel attendance and strict adherence to a series of rules that forbade swearing, drinking, and fornicating. I bent those rules only very slightly.

The summer after my sophomore year of college, I stumbled into a job as a youth minister at a church not too far from where I grew up. It was supposed to be a summer internship. I stayed for three years. Soon after, at the tender age of twenty-three, I was preaching every Sunday to another small congregation not too far from the campus where I was pursuing a graduate degree in political science. After a year behind the pulpit, I tried to leave the ministry, but it didn't last long. I then became the interim pastor of First Baptist Church of Mount Vernon at age twenty-four and was there for over seventeen years.

I'd never felt called to be a minister. I was too scared to say no. And now those twenty years of serving congregations in the American Baptist tradition were coming to an unceremonious end. Not that I was ever that good at the job, honestly. When it came to the traditional metrics of attendance, number of baptisms, and giving, my two decades as a member of the clergy had been an abject failure.

That first church where I youth pastored was a shadow of its former self. On a good Sunday, there would be 150 in worship when I was on staff. Now, it was about a third the size and there had been no youth group to speak of for at least a decade. A Google search I did when I couldn't sleep one night informed me that the second church where I pastored had closed its doors and sold off all its assets, with the building razed to put in a housing development. And my latest church wasn't too terribly far behind. A congregation that numbered three hundred in the 1960s was soon to be extinguished forever. I may be the least successful Baptist pastor in history.

Even so, I loved these kinds of churches because they were exactly where my faith was—always questioning, welcoming to doubters, inviting newcomers. After being raised in an evangelical tradition that made everything about the world black and white, I went to college and realized there was a lot more gray out there. Learning about other religious traditions made me question my own. The way I often describe it is, I went to college believing a whole lot of things a little bit and left believing a few things a whole lot. My faith was complicated and ever evolving.

The American Baptist Church was a perfect fit for someone like me. It's a tradition dating back to the Civil War. When the majority of Baptists in the South wanted to allow missionaries to own slaves, abolitionist Baptists broke away and formed the Northern Baptist Convention, which was later rebranded the American Baptist Church. The denomination has always emphasized a middle path. A local church decides who its pastor can be. If the pastor is a woman, so be it. If a church wants to affirm LGBTQ+ individuals, the national headquarters can't do anything about it. For American Baptists, each believer gets to make up their own mind about how to interpret the Bible. It isn't the pastor's job to tell them what to think.

Because American Baptists tend to be more moderate than evangelical traditions, they are often classified by scholars of American religion as a mainline denomination. But as we'll soon see, churches that occupy this middle space are quickly becoming few and far between. The American Baptists are in a very similar situation to that of the United Methodists, the Episcopalians, the United Church of Christ, and the Evangelical Lutheran Church in America. At one point, about half of all Americans were part of this moderate, mainline tradition. In twenty or thirty years, if current trends continue as predicted, the mainline tradition will largely be extinct across many parts of the United States.

This tectonic shift in American religion has happened so slowly and methodically that most Americans don't even know about it. While the average American has likely heard about the Southern Baptist Convention and its stance on topics like women in ministry, when I use the term "mainline Protestant" outside a group of religion nerds, I get a lot of quizzical looks. Many Americans just aren't aware that nonevangelical Christianity exists and that it used to dominate the American church landscape.

What used to be nothing more than a thought exercise—where will I worship after my church closes—has become a very stark reality. I am going to be in an incredibly difficult spot when First Baptist closes its doors. I am a Christian, but I have a hard time embracing the certainty that is so pervasive among my more conservative brethren. In fact, when I hear bold pronouncements from the pulpit of an evangelical church, my mind always conjures two questions: How can this person be so sure of themself? and Why can't I believe in something as much as the people sitting next to me?

And I know I am not alone.

No Place for Moderates

Forty years ago, someone looking for a new church would have had a range of options available to them. Most rural towns had a number of evangelical churches, but they typically also had a vibrant Methodist, Episcopal, or Lutheran church in the community. There was a place to feel welcomed and embraced no matter how much or how little one believed in Jesus Christ that particular Sunday—or how one cast their ballot on Election Day. But that's no longer the case. The religious landscape of the United States has never looked starker than it does today. There are huge geographical swaths of America where the only place a Protestant can worship on a Sunday morning is an evangelical church that takes a literalist view of the Bible and believes that women have no role in spiritual leadership. The vibrant religious marketplace that was pervasive for most of US history has been replaced by a type of faith that certainly appeals to a subset of the country but is objectionable, if not downright repulsive, to a significant number of Americans.

In short, American religion has become an "all or none" proposition—conservative evangelical religion or none at all. This leaves tens of millions of theological and political moderates with no place to find community and spiritual edification, or to work collectively to solve societal problems.

There's been a tremendous amount of media coverage about the rapid rise and deleterious impacts of political polarization over the last several years. The data is clear: Democrats have become more liberal, and Republicans are lurching further to the right. As a trained political scientist, I can tell you that this is not just a perception but an empirical reality.

Yet a twin trend that has received less media coverage is that there's been a tremendous amount of polarization in American religion as well. While political moderates have gone the way of the dodo in statehouses and the nation's capital, the same thing has been happening in houses of worship. American churches are more likely to be split along our red and blue lines. Churchgoers are far less likely today to worship alongside people who vote differently than they do. And religion itself is increasingly coded as right-wing.

I have spent the last fifteen years as a quantitative scholar of American religion. It is safe to say that I have made *a lot* of graphs about the contours of the religious landscape in the United States. My research has led me to an important and unnerving conclusion about the future of faith in this country.

There are many people on the far right of American religiosity, including groups like white evangelicals, traditional Catholics, Muslims, and Latter-day Saints. And a growing number of people claim no religious affiliation—such as atheists, agnostics, and those who describe themselves as spiritual but not religious. But fewer and fewer people inhabit the middle of the American religious landscape. These are the kind of people who used to sit shoulder to shoulder in the pews of churches just like mine on a Sunday morning. These kinds of moderate churches could be found in communities big and small, in the Midwest, New England, and the Bible Belt. These Episcopal, Presbyterian, and Methodist houses of worship were made up of people from a variety of educational, class, and political backgrounds. They were excellent incubators of social capital. And now many are on their last legs.

In the United States, two distinct sides of American religion currently exist. On one end of the spectrum are people who are absolutely certain that their belief system is the correct one; many of them believe that the laws of the country should reflect the theological precepts laid out in their interpretation of the Bible (or Torah or Qur'an). Meanwhile, on the other side of the spectrum is a growing number of people who not only have walked away from any religious tradition but also feel that religion is a caustic force in American society and that the government should remove any special protections that exist for houses of worship. (There are churches that don't fall on either end of the political continuum, as we will see in the upcoming pages. However, these churches are quite literally vanishing and in many parts of the United States are almost impossible to find.)

Yet in the middle of all this are tens of millions of Americans who miss the way that a significant portion of religion used to be—moderate, sensible, pragmatic, and unifying. The kind of churches where pastors didn't yell about eternal damnation every Sunday but instead focused on encouraging congregants to love their neighbors and make the world a bit better for those around them. These churches used to be the dominant force in American Protestant Christianity; today they are largely marginalized from the broader cultural discourse.

But this is not just an argument from a Christian author to a Christian audience bemoaning the decline of religion. I believe the stakes are much higher than that.

A Problem Facing Us All

The share of Americans who say that they never attend church services grew from forty-five million in 2008 to eighty-five million in 2022.[1] And thousands of churches are going to close across the United States over the next several decades. However, after reading hundreds of academic articles on the sociology of religion, I've learned that this isn't just a church or church people problem. The decline of American religion will have deleterious impacts on every single facet of American society. The decline of the church is a problem not just for religiously inclined people—it's a problem for us all.

By driving out the moderates from American religion, we have created a divide in which a whole bunch of people on each side are convinced that those on the other side are immoral or bigots. Many white evangelicals are convinced that anyone who votes for a Democrat is a baby killer, while many atheists believe that anyone who supports a Republican must be a racist. Outright animus toward those who are different has only been accelerated by the fact that so few of us have any real interactions with people who have a political or religious worldview different from ours.

Religion, at its very best, can tamp down feelings of distrust, disenchantment, and disconnection. At their best, religious institutions are places where people from different economic backgrounds and political affiliations can sit side by side and worship together. Families have the chance to make friends with others in the same situation over a potluck meal or during church league softball. Now, many houses of worship have become partisan echo chambers where pastors do little more than reinforce the beliefs of the people in the pews, to hearty amens and nodding approval from the congregations. Instead of churches being engines of social capital generation and catalysts for building trust and tolerance, the growing polarization of American religion has left us lonelier, angrier, sicker, and more divided (both economically and politically) than ever before.

The purpose of this book is threefold. First, in part 1, I'll take you on a tour of the American religious landscape over the last fifty years in a broad sweep. Understanding the trajectory of Protestant Christianity (both evangelical and mainline), Catholicism, and the rise of the nones is absolutely essential for understanding how and why religious polarization has become so extreme. This will happen in chapters 2 through 5. Think of this section as a diagnosis.

Part 2 digs deeper into the question of why, offering an explanation. Yes, the nones have risen dramatically and the mainline has collapsed, but what factors led to those trend lines moving in opposite directions? Think of it as an autopsy of sorts. Chapter 6 expands the polarization thesis to more than politics. The American church has become filled with people with good educations and solid incomes—unintentionally shunning tens of millions of people who did not do everything "right." Chapter 7 tries to understand what factors in the 1990s led to this rapid polarization, and chapter 8 describes its logical endpoint: religion being reduced to little more than a tribal identity.

Finally, in part 3, I want to leave you with a prescription for how we get out of this morass. While a lot of the charts and graphs in this book will make you feel pessimistic about the future, there's a significant amount of data in chapter 9 that can offer hope—that suggests that the average American is a lot more moderate, pragmatic, and sensible than they are given credit for. Which leads to chapter 10's consideration of how that huge number of people in the middle can understand their role in a functional religious marketplace and how they can help build democracy, not tear it down.

While most of this book is primarily from my vantage point as a social scientist, the last couple chapters take on a more pastoral tone to help readers grasp how they can tangibly respond to the concerning trends. There are ways to correct these problems and return American religion to what it looked like just a few decades ago, but it will take work. A concerted effort by religious leaders and laypeople could bring about a more diverse and vibrant religious landscape than is currently available to the millions of Americans who want to be part of a faith community but just can't find a house of worship that makes sense to them.

When I preach my last sermon at First Baptist Church, I'm not sure I'll be able to find a suitable community of faith. It's not my fault that American religion has changed so much during my lifetime, but it is most certainly my problem to face. Just like it's a problem for tens of millions of others who are in the same position. I know it would be much simpler for me to just stay home that next Sunday and the Sunday after that. If I understand anything about myself as I move into middle age, it's simply this: I am much more inclined to choose the easiest route, not the most personally edifying one. So this book will become a way to encourage myself to do the right thing, even as it calls to you, reader, to consider how you should move forward.

PART 1

FIVE DECADES OF RELIGIOUS POLARIZATION

2

Evangelicals

THE BIG TAKEAWAYS

- Despite the rapid religious decline in the United States, evangelicalism is still incredibly robust.
- White evangelicalism is more politically unified now than at any point in the last fifty years.

There may be no word more loaded in the study of American religion than "evangelical."

For some, it's a rallying cry, a way to quickly situate themselves in social, political, and theological space. For others, it's an epithet, denoting individuals who advocate for causes and hold beliefs that they vehemently disagree with. In many ways, the word is polarization personified. Just uttering the word can have almost a Red Sea feeling to it, evoking the moment when Moses stood on the shore, stretched out his hand, and parted the waters. Some people in the room will immediately feel a warmth and belonging, while others will almost visibly wince.

What a significant number of Americans don't know is that it hasn't always been this way. In the scope of American religious and political history, evangelicalism has become a shorthand for a specific political worldview only very recently.

Many historians have traced evangelicalism in the United States back to the precolonial period. Many of us know the story of the Pilgrims arriving on American shores in search of freedom to practice their religion in the way they saw fit. What is often less well understood is that the Pilgrims come out of the Puritan tradition—which held to the theological belief that it is impossible to live a life of piety and devotion while being surrounded by sinful people. Thus, the Pilgrims felt compelled to make the perilous journey to the New World to set up a faith community that was separate from sinful behavior, something that was not possible in England.

From that point forward, evangelicalism always had a foothold on American shores. However, the momentum of this type of theology rapidly accelerated during the First Great Awakening, which took place in the 1730s and 1740s in many of the most populous parts of colonial America. Taking on many of the motifs of the Puritanism and Pietism that had been imported by the Pilgrims, preachers like Jonathan Edwards, George Whitefield, and John Wesley called the colonists to repent of their sins and seek salvation through the atoning acts of Jesus Christ. While it's hard to come to precise estimates of those who became evangelicals during this movement, the Congregational churches in New England reported 25,000 to 50,000 new members out of a total population of 340,000.[1] In other words, evangelicalism was on the march long before Thomas Jefferson sat down to write the Declaration of Independence.

The Second Great Awakening began during the last few years of the eighteenth century and continued through the early part of the nineteenth century. It was much larger in scope than the previous revivalistic movement. While pastors like Edwards and

Whitefield had implored the colonists to seek personal salvation and individual piety, the second movement was more focused on social reform. The seeds of the campaign for women's suffrage were planted during the Second Great Awakening, and many of the strongest voices in the abolitionist movement used religious language and imagery to push for an end to slavery.

Yet even as the United States moved into the twentieth century, evangelical Christians didn't have a connection to any specific political party. Other factors like region, economic class, and country of origin were much more important contributors to vote choice on Election Day than a personal relationship with Jesus Christ. And for many evangelicals, avoiding politics was the ideal way to practice personal piety. Which party won the White House was of little consequence in the pursuit of living a life of chastity, charity, and devotion to God. In fact, any time that evangelicals tried to make a significant impact on the larger culture, it often resulted in ridicule, mockery, and derision from mainstream society.

The Scopes Monkey Trial stands as a clear example of this. The state of Tennessee had passed legislation that banned the teaching of evolution in public schools at the behest of many evangelicals living in the state. Less than six weeks later, John Scopes, a high school teacher, decided to violate the law to test the legality of the statute. He was charged with a crime and went on trial in the summer of 1925, with the eyes of the nation and the world squarely focused on the tiny town of Dayton, Tennessee.

It quickly became apparent that what was on trial was not Darwin's evolutionary theory but the proper role of religion in public life.

William Jennings Bryan, the special prosecutor hired by the state, may have been the most prominent evangelical of the day. And Clarence Darrow, the attorney who was appointed to defend Scopes, was likely the most high-profile atheist in the country. At the height of the courtroom drama, Bryan was called to the witness stand to defend his view that the Bible is the literal Word of God.

When Darrow got Bryan to admit that he believed the earth did, in fact, stand still as described in the book of Joshua, the media coverage was brutal.

Perhaps the most biting of all commentators was a newspaperman, H. L. Mencken. When Bryan died just a few days after the verdict was handed down, Mencken excoriated him in an obituary: "He seemed only a poor clod like those around him, deluded by a childish theology, full of an almost pathological hatred of all learning, all human dignity, all beauty, all fine and noble things."[2]

Many evangelicals read those words as aimed directly at themselves. They quickly realized that continuing to engage the larger culture and shape public policy would only result in more mockery. Many of them retreated from public life, content with the notion that they could focus on their personal quest for purification while the rest of the world went to hell.

Religion scholar Karen Armstrong describes the post-Scopes period this way: "During their time in the political wilderness, the fundamentalists became more radical, nursing a deep grievance against mainstream American culture. Subsequent history would show that when a fundamentalist movement is attacked, it almost invariably becomes more aggressive, bitter, and excessive."[3] Thus, the political might of millions of American evangelicals was largely unrealized for half a century. They were certainly not a coherent voting bloc that either party could count on in large numbers. While there were white evangelicals who opposed the racial integration of public schools in the wake of *Brown v. Board of Education*, the protests against that US Supreme Court decision were largely devoid of religious language or imagery.

When looking at the partisan composition of white evangelicals beginning in the early 1970s, the peculiarity of the current moment comes into sharper focus. In 1972, 59 percent of white evangelicals identified as Democrats, 32 percent as Republicans, and about 9 percent as independents. Then the trend lines for Republicans and Democrats quickly began to converge. By 1984,

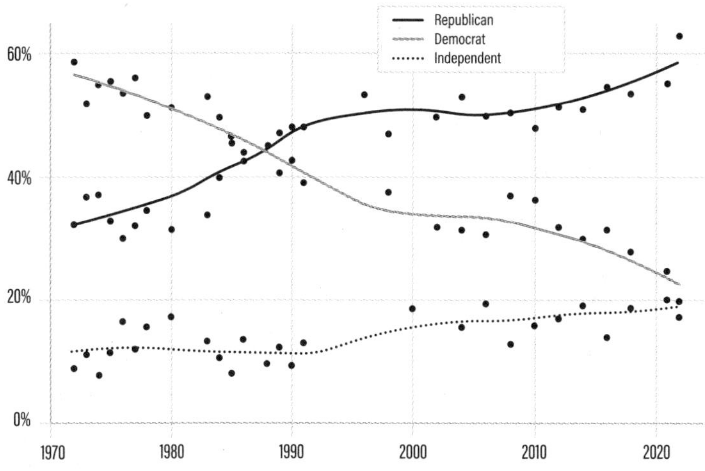

Figure 2.1 The political partisanship of white evangelicals, 1972–2022

50 percent of white evangelicals identified as Democrats, and the Republicans had increased their share to 40 percent. Just five years later, the largest percentage of white evangelicals aligned with the GOP (see fig. 2.1).

What's easy to miss in figure 2.1 is the fifteen-year period between 1993 and 2008. The share of Republicans did not substantially change—it hovered right around 50 percent. Meanwhile, the percentage of Democrats kept declining, while the share who identified as independents rose by about 5 percentage points. How to explain this? It's likely that a contingent of white evangelicals who used to align with the Democrats had walked away from that label but were as yet unwilling to embrace a Republican identity.

However, that began to shift after the 2008 election of Barack Obama. There is a clear and discernible inflection point in the trend lines beginning with data collected in 2010 and beyond. About 49 percent of white evangelicals were Republicans during this period. By 2016, the number had risen to 55 percent and then jumped a full eight percentage points by 2022, settling in at 63 percent. That's an increase of fourteen percentage points in just twelve years. Meanwhile, white evangelical Democrats became increasingly hard to find, making up just 17 percent of the sample, which was even lower than the evangelicals who polled as independents at 20 percent.

One way that political scientists measure polarization is quite simple: find the difference in percentages of those who identify with each of the two major parties. So if a group is 45 percent Democrat and 45 percent Republican, the polarization score is zero. If a part of the population is 80 percent Republican and 20 percent Democrat, its polarization score is sixty. From this perspective, it makes no difference which party has a larger share; the difference in the sizes of the percentages is the more important metric.

When one calculates the polarization score for white evangelicals over the past fifty years, the uniqueness of the present moment becomes readily apparent (see fig. 2.2).

In the early 1970s, the polarization of white evangelicals was fairly high. It remained close to twenty-five through 1977. However,

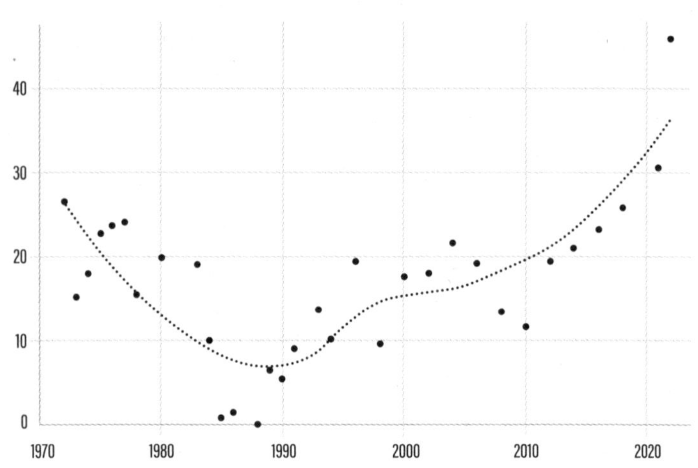

Figure 2.2 Polarization score of white evangelicals, 1972–2022

it began dropping rapidly in the decade to come. It was clearly below ten by 1984, and there were single-year estimates of this polarization score that were incredibly low—it averaged just 0.8 between 1985 and 1988. This means that if one attended a random white evangelical church in the late 1980s, it would not be at all surprising to see a Democrat sitting next to a Republican on a typical Sunday. Obviously, there were regional differences, but the white evangelical movement as a whole did not have a distinct political tilt.

However, from that point forward, the polarization score began to shoot up. By 2000, it was around fifteen, and by 2010, it had increased another five points. It's fair to say that the estimates from the last ten years of the General Social Survey (the most widely respected survey of American religion, administered by NORC at the University of Chicago) only point in the direction of rapidly increasing polarization. In 2018, the polarization score was nearly the same as it was in 1972, but this time in the opposite direction—Republicans outnumbering Democrats. But the last two years of data point to something else entirely. The polarization score was thirty-one in 2021 and then forty-six in 2022. This means that, unlike in previous eras, if one attended a random white evangelical church today, it would be highly *unlikely* to find a Democrat sitting next to a Republican on a typical Sunday. The white evangelical movement has never been more politically homogeneous than it is right now.

That also comes through when looking at the presidential vote choice among white evangelicals beginning in 1960. It's fair to say that white evangelicals, on balance, have favored Republicans over Democrats on Election Day for the last six decades. But it's also fair to conclude that white evangelicals weren't overwhelmingly casting ballots for Republicans through most of the past sixty years. For instance, Gerald Ford earned 58 percent of the white evangelical vote in 1976, but Ronald Reagan would then improve on this in both 1980 and 1988.

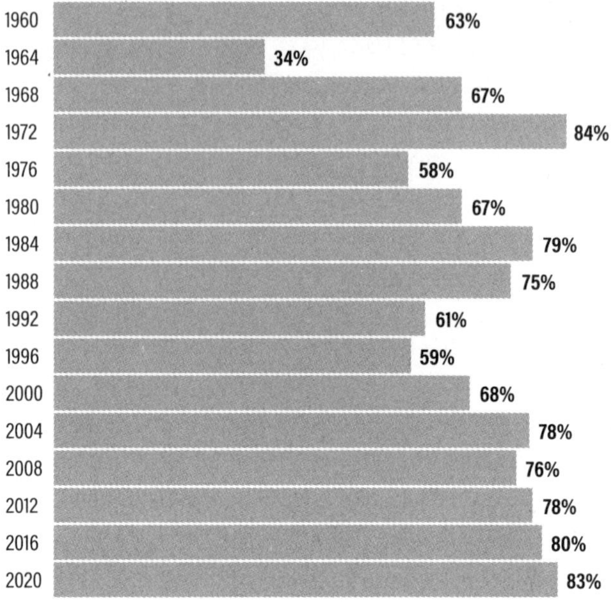

Figure 2.3 Share of white evangelicals who voted for the Republican candidate for president, 1960–2020

However, the election and reelection of Bill Clinton in 1992 and 1996 are instructive (see fig. 2.3). In both cycles, just three in five white evangelicals cast ballots for the Republican candidate.

Those two elections, and the contest between George W. Bush and Al Gore, were especially formative for me. I was born in 1982 and thus was just learning about politics and the political process when Clinton was impeached for lying under oath about his coercive sexual relationship with Monica Lewinsky. My high school years were completely consumed by evangelical Christianity. I wore Christian T-shirts, listened to contemporary Christian music almost exclusively, and looked forward to attending church camp every year. So the discussion around Clinton's sexual sins was something that I heard about from both the pulpit and the pews in my Southern Baptist congregation.

But looking back on that moment, I am struck by how the rhetoric that I heard about presidents being moral leaders did not really translate into white evangelicals completely rejecting Clinton and the Democrats in that next election cycle. At the national level, Gore did lose ground for Democrats among white evangelicals compared with the two previous elections, but in comparison, Gore did no worse than Jimmy Carter had done among white evangelicals in 1980.

Because I was attending college, I voted absentee at the Marion County Courthouse in my very first presidential election. That small southern Illinois county, with a population of just about forty thousand, was about as politically diverse as it got during the 2000 election. Of the 16,308 votes cast, Gore received 8,068 of them; Bush's total was slightly higher, at 8,240. In percentage terms, the Republican beat the Democrat by a single percentage point. So, my experience as a white evangelical in rural America was not one where I felt that it was a God-given duty to cast a ballot for only the GOP, and it looks like many in my strongly evangelical county felt the same.

The data makes clear that the 2000 election marked a completely different era. From that point forward, white evangelical voters began to vote in lockstep. Democrat John Kerry won just 22 percent of that voting bloc just four years later. And little has changed the past five election cycles. Sure, Obama did slightly better for the Democrats, but he still lost three-quarters of the white evangelical vote in his landslide election in 2008. Republican Mitt Romney did two points better in 2012 than his party's John McCain had in 2008, and then Donald Trump took it one step farther. In the 2016 and 2020 election cycles, for each white evangelical who pulled the proverbial lever for the Democrat, four white evangelicals did the same for the Republican.

In the five presidential elections from 2000 to 2020, the share of white evangelicals who supported the Republican was 79 percent. It was 68 percent in the five elections before that. It was just 62 percent in the five elections spanning 1964 through 1980. Any way you slice it, white evangelicals are more politically unified today than at any point in the last six decades. And that unanimity also shows up in my home county. Recall that Al Gore got nearly half the votes cast in Marion County, Illinois, in 2000. In the 2020 contest between Joe Biden and Trump, the Democratic candidate earned 26 percent of the vote. My county went from being one Republican per one Democrat to three Republicans per one Democrat in the span of just two decades. It's impossible to think that this doesn't relate, at least in some part, to the growing political conservatism in white evangelical Christianity.

The Effects of Political Homogeneity

When such a large social group becomes politically unified, downstream effects inevitably follow. It may have driven some people away from evangelicalism, such as those whose politics were slightly right of center but not conservative enough to satisfy some of the louder voices in evangelical churches and communities. But a reverse motion could also be true. Some people who were not particularly religious but were ideologically to the right may have been drawn into a church that provided them a theological justification for their preexisting political views.

If we trace the size of the evangelical movement over the last five decades, we see a nuanced portrait emerge that doesn't fully support either hypothesis.

Figure 2.4 shows that in 1972 just 17 percent of American adults were aligned with an evangelical denomination, such as the Southern Baptist Convention. By 1980, 24 percent of adults were in evangelical churches. What is especially striking is that from 1983 to 1993, the share of evangelicals jumped nearly seven percentage points in a single decade. The numerical peak of the movement in the United States was in 1993, when about three in ten adults were evangelicals. What is fascinating is that if one references the

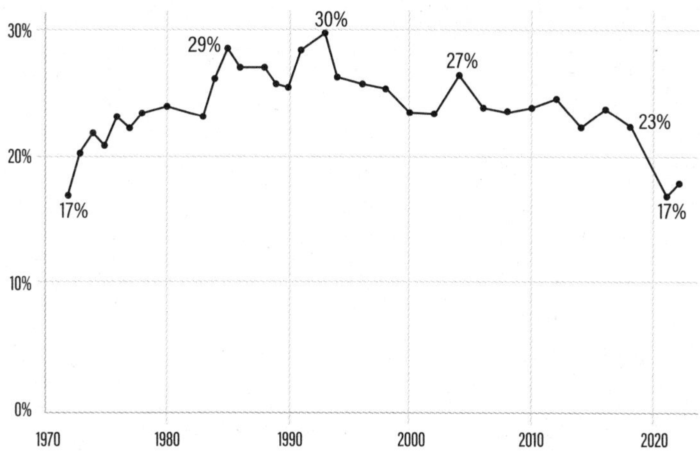

Figure 2.4 Share of the population that is evangelical by denominational affiliation, 1972–2022

graph that tracks the polarization score of evangelicals (fig. 2.2), this is when the religious group was the most politically diverse—the share of Republicans and the share of Democrats were nearly equal.

By the year 2000, the share of evangelicals in the sample had returned to 24 percent, which was essentially the same percentage it had been twenty years earlier. Over the next ten to fifteen years, the evangelical portion of America was remarkably stable, averaging about 23 percent a year until the last few years, when it began to decline again. In the 2021 sample, about 17 percent were evangelicals; however, the number rebounded slightly to 18 percent in 2022. (One thing that clouds interpretation of the statistics from both 2021 and 2022 is that the General Social Survey had to fundamentally change its collection process due to the COVID-19 pandemic, and this significantly affected several measures. So the six-point drop from 2018 to 2021 may be a statistical aberration.)

However, if one traces the political trajectory of evangelicals against their relative size over the last five decades, it's hard to conclude that their significant lurch to the right negatively affected their numbers. For instance, evangelicalism was twice as politically polarized in 2018 as it was in 2000, yet the total share of adults who aligned with an evangelical tradition remained largely unchanged during that period. Said more plainly: The data doesn't suggest that becoming more politically conservative equated to a net negative for evangelicalism's share of the population.

A pair of Pew Research Center surveys lend credence to this conclusion. Surveyors contacted individuals immediately after the 2016 presidential election and followed up with those same people right after the 2020 presidential contest, asking questions about their political views and religious affiliation. Among the sample collected in 2016, the share who self-identified as evangelical was 25 percent. Four years later, that increased to 29 percent. There was one clear factor in the data that increased the likelihood of assuming an evangelical identity: a warm feeling toward Donald Trump. When looking at only people who did not identify as evangelical in 2016, 16 percent of those with warm feelings toward Trump began identifying as evangelical by 2020. Only 1 percent of the new evangelicals expressed cooler feelings toward the president.

Many people believe that Trump's election and reelection and the continuing move toward conservatism among white evangelical Christianity has made the term radioactive to a significant swath of the population. While that may be true to an extent, it's also true that the marriage between the Republican Party and evangelical Christianity may have made the tradition more attractive to a different group of people. There are people who have begun attending evangelical churches more for their partisan leanings than their theological views.

In fact, the continuing march toward the right in terms of vote choice is reflected in several key policy positions, abortion chief among them (see fig. 2.5). It's widely understood that white evangelicals have been consistently opposed to a woman's right to obtain an abortion, and the data supports this. The General

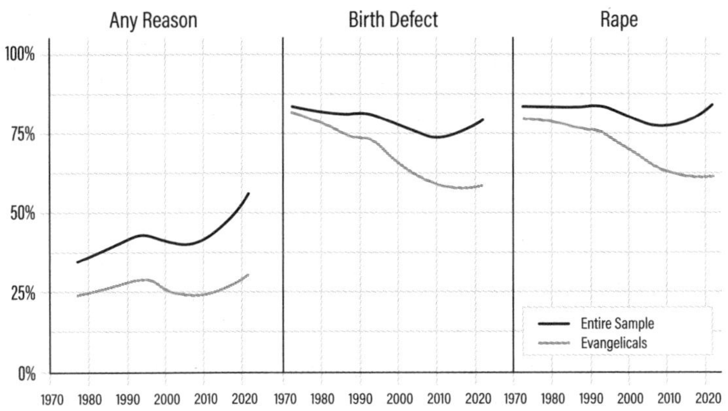

Figure 2.5 Share of the population in favor of abortion access in multiple scenarios, 1972–2022

Social Survey began asking respondents about supporting access to a legal abortion for any reason in 1977. In that survey, just a quarter of white evangelicals were in favor. In the latest data, this increased only marginally to about 30 percent. When this group is compared with the general public, an interesting story emerges. In 1978, just 37 percent of all Americans were in favor of abortion for any reason—only seven points higher than evangelicals. However, in 2022, that percentage had increased to 57 percent—which means that the gap between the groups now stands at twenty-seven percentage points. That's an all-time high.

However, where the real movement on abortion has occurred is in more nuanced scenarios that are not necessarily in the camp of an "elective procedure." For instance, what about a woman's ability to obtain an abortion if the pregnancy occurred due to rape or if the baby has a serious birth defect? In the early 1970s, white evangelicals overwhelmingly supported legal access to an abortion in both cases, at around 80 percent in favor of an exception in both cases. On these two questions, evangelicals were not substantively out of step with the general public.

That's clearly no longer the case. Over the last fifty years, evangelicals have become less permissive of abortion in these situations. In the case of a severe birth defect and rape, just 60 percent of evangelicals favor abortion now. In comparison, 85 percent of the general public would allow abortion in the case of rape (the highest percentage in thirty years), and 80 percent would allow abortion when there's a severe fetal defect, which is higher than any point in the last twenty years. Again, the gap between these two trend lines has never been larger than it is right now.

Beyond their conservative bona fides on abortion and other social issues, the evidence, based on several metrics that gauge religiosity, suggests that evangelicals have never been more devout than they are at this present moment. For instance, church attendance has never been higher for people who align with an evangelical tradition, even going back to the 1970s (see fig. 2.6).

In 1972, about 42 percent of all evangelicals reported that they attended religious services nearly every week or more. That percentage has only increased over time. By the late 1980s, it was north of 45 percent, and right around 2010, half of evangelicals said that they were in church every week. The percentage has continued to increase from there and may continue to increase even more rapidly. The last two times that the General Social Survey was conducted, in 2021 and 2022, the share of evangelicals who reported weekly attendance was above 57 percent. That's fifteen percentage points higher than the average attendance rates of evangelicals in the 1970s.

For comparison, the share of adult Americans who were attending religious services nearly every week was about 35 percent in the 1970s and dropped incrementally over the next several decades. It was right around 30 percent by the early 2010s and declined even more in recent years. In 2018, 27 percent of the sample attended weekly; it was 25 percent in 2021 and 22 percent in 2022—the lowest ever recorded. This data is the reason it's difficult to answer a straightforward question like "Is religion in decline?" Yes, it clearly is among the general population. But a parallel truth is

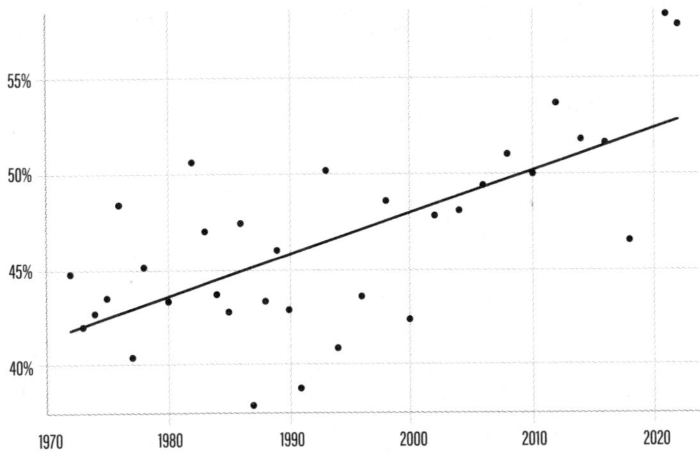

Figure 2.6 Share of white evangelicals who attend church nearly every week or more, 1972–2022

that the attendance rate of evangelicals has never been higher than it is right now, increasing about fifteen percentage points over the last five decades. At least when it comes to church attendance, the split between evangelicals and mainstream Americans has never been wider.

It's also the case that those who are in the pews are more theologically unified than ever before. It's notoriously difficult to assess religious belief by using survey questions, but the General Social Survey has been asking people about their views of the Bible since the late 1980s. Respondents are given three options: (1) the Bible is the Word of God and should be taken as literally true, (2) the Bible is inspired by God but should not be taken as literally true, or (3) the Bible is a book of fables and stories. Biblical literalism has always been a key hallmark of the evangelical movement in the United States, but the data points to the fact that not all adherents would agree that the Bible should be taken literally.

In figure 2.7, we see that in 1988 about 68 percent of weekly-attending white evangelicals took a literalist position regarding the Bible. Over time, that percentage has increased, albeit slowly. At

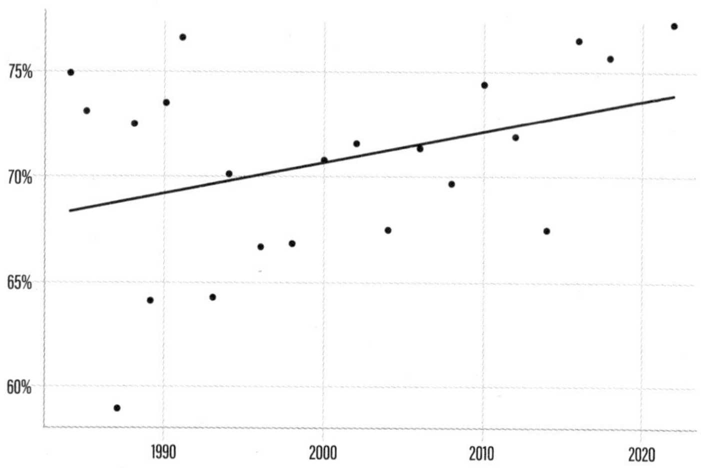

Figure 2.7 Share of weekly-attending white evangelicals who believe the Bible is literally true, 1988–2022

least 70 percent of active white evangelicals were literalists by the late 1990s. That increased to 72 percent by 2012, and in the last several survey collections the percentages have moved even higher. Since 2018, three-quarters of weekly-attending white evangelicals have said that the Bible should be taken as the literal Word of God. In other words, not only are evangelicals more likely to attend religious services today than at any point since 1972, but those who are attending are also more likely to take the most conservative view of the Bible.

It's hard to look at this data and think that evangelicalism is declining in the United States. Yes, the share of Americans who are white evangelicals is falling, in part because the portion of the population that is white is in decline. However, the overall share of adults who are evangelicals today is the same as it was in 1972. The number of evangelical Christians in the United States in 2022 could be estimated at sixty million—that's just about the same number of evangelicals in the country twenty years ago. So, numerically speaking, outside of the Catholic Church, evangelicalism is easily the largest religious movement in the United States.

And—important for the purposes of this book—evangelicalism has become more theologically and politically homogeneous today than at any moment in recent history. The overall political polarization of white evangelicalism is higher than it's been in the last fifty years. At the same time, the portion of all evangelicals who participate in weekly worship is trending upward and those who are sitting in the pews are more likely to be biblical literalists now than twenty or thirty years ago.

If one attended an evangelical church in the 1970s or 1980s, it was generally just as likely one would be sitting next to a Democrat as a Republican. Also, while there were plenty of biblical literalists in those pews during that time, there was a sizable minority who believed that the Bible was inspired but should not be read literally. That's no longer the case.

The portrait that emerges from all this data is quite clear: A movement that used to be fairly diverse politically and theologically has become what it is often caricatured as in the mainstream media—a whole lot of theologically conservative Republicans. Yet this has not caused a huge decline in their size or influence in the American religious, political, or cultural landscape. If evangelicals have learned any lessons from the last fifty years, one of them is that you aren't penalized for moving toward a political monoculture.

Evangelicalism has always thrived by living in the inherent tension of being "in the world but not of it." It's a phrase that is often offered to young believers to help them understand their need to engage culture without being assimilated into that larger culture. Unfortunately, the rightward turn in evangelical politics has made it even more difficult for the movement to engage the average American. Instead of portraying itself as just a bit different from the dominant culture, evangelicalism over the last forty years has almost returned to the model of William Jennings Bryan—a man who may have won the courtroom battle but certainly lost the culture war.

Now, instead of trying to find areas of cultural commonalities, the loudest voices in evangelicalism have become convinced that the only way to maintain the movement is by cloistering it in an increasingly conservative brand of right-wing politics. Seeking an end to in vitro fertilization, barring women from any type of pastoral role, and being almost completely unified behind the Republican Party have created an environment where any pastor who tries to find common cause with those outside the evangelical tribe faces potential ostracism. This makes bringing new converts into the flock much more difficult, but it also makes governing nearly untenable. When politicians are incentivized to dig in their heels and not compromise on any issue (big or small), just passing a budget becomes a nearly impossible task. For evangelicalism, "compromise" has become a dirty word, yet in the world of democratic politics, it's an absolute necessity.

3

Mainline Protestants

THE BIG TAKEAWAYS

- Mainline Protestant Christianity used to be the largest and most influential religious tradition in the United States. Now it's quickly headed for extinction.
- Against stereotypes of ultraprogressivism, the mainline has been a politically diverse religious tradition, with Republicans and Democrats sitting side by side on Sunday morning.

Anyone observing American religion over the last several decades and its impact on politics may think only of hot-button issues such as abortion and same-sex marriage. But the influence Protestants have had in American life goes much deeper. Many of the most momentous social movements in US history—those that abolished slavery, ended the Gilded Age, and fought to ensure equal treatment of individuals regardless of race—were spearheaded by Protestant organizations.

In the last decade of the nineteenth century and into the early twentieth, many Protestants began to embrace what became known as the social gospel. Protestant theologians and pastors argued that the aim of Christians should be not merely to transform individual lives through evangelism but also to make the world a better place. This was more than a theoretical pursuit; quality of life had deteriorated significantly for the millions who had moved into industrial centers across the Northeast. Urban centers could not keep up with the growing influx of eager workers, leading to overcrowded tenement buildings, a rapid increase in diseases due to a lack of sanitation, and growing income inequality as factory owners were reaping huge rewards while workers were often paid meager wages that kept them and their families in poverty.

In response to these social crises, several denominations worked together to form the Federal Council of Churches in 1908. The council became one of the key organizations behind many of the changes in American society during the Progressive Era. The Federal Council of Churches adopted the "Social Creeds of the Churches," which focused on issues like workers' rights, child labor laws, and living wages for all who worked full-time in the thousands of factories that had sprouted up during the Industrial Revolution. Many of these efforts brought lasting changes to labor laws and improved living conditions for the average American.

Eventually, the zeal for the social gospel began to wane as the movement faced a major setback in the repeal of Prohibition, a policy that had strong support from the members of the Federal Council of Churches. Over time this group added new members, merged with other organizations, and in 1950 changed its name to the National Council of Churches (NCC). Beyond the previously mentioned social reforms of the Progressive Era, the NCC has a legacy of counterbalancing evangelical Christianity in the United States. The consensus among scholars of American religion is that the NCC's largest majority-white denominations are part of a tradition called "the mainline."

Many historians of American religion believe this name derives from the existence of a number of prominent, white, well-to-do churches along the Pennsylvania Railroad Main Line in suburban Philadelphia. This accurately describes the modern conception of mainline Protestants—that they are overwhelmingly white and highly educated, with above-average incomes. For instance, essayist H. L. Mencken once wrote, "Most Americans, when they accumulate money, climb the golden spires of the nearest Episcopal Church."[1] The Episcopal Church may be the prototypical mainline denomination in the United States, but the mainline tradition also includes groups like the United Methodist Church, the United Church of Christ, the Disciples of Christ, the Evangelical Lutheran Church in America, the American Baptist Church, and the Presbyterian Church (USA).

If there is one phrase to describe the mainline tradition, it's not "radical liberal" but rather "middle of the road." Its members tend to be a bit less dogmatic than their evangelical cousins. While mainline Protestants do hold to many of the core tenets of the Christian faith, articulated in statements like the Apostles' and Nicene Creeds, their beliefs and preaching tend to be less bombastic. Their worship services are often a bit more formal and typically include hymns with piano or organ accompaniment. The laity also tends to favor a more moderate flavor of politics that focuses on consensus and pragmatism. Because members of the mainline are less strident in their theological positions, their politics seems less dependent on their views of the Bible or interpretations of specific passages of Scripture.

I grew up knowing nothing of the mainline. It's a term I didn't learn until I became a student at a small Christian college and began expanding my horizons beyond the Southern Baptist church of my youth.

I fell headlong into the mainline largely by accident. The summer after my sophomore year of college, I needed a job. In a class I took on the philosophy of youth ministry, our professor mentioned a Baptist church about twenty miles from my hometown that was looking for a youth ministry intern. My only other option for summer employment was working as an overnight stocker at a big box store. After a short interview process, the church hired me to work with its middle and high school students through the end of August.

The church was First Baptist of Centralia, Illinois. I grew up in First Baptist of Salem, Illinois. It had to be pretty similar, right? My first clue that not all Baptist churches were the same came when I began thumbing through a directory of other local churches in the denomination and noticed that some of the senior pastors were women. This was certainly not what I was used to. I quickly ascertained that my new employer was aligned with the American Baptist Church, a denomination that had split with the Southern Baptists over the issue of slavery and welcomed women in the pulpit.

As I stayed longer in the mainline, several characteristics of the tradition made profound impacts on my personal life and my career. My first discovery was that the mainline was more welcoming of doubters—which is exactly what I was. I never felt truly at home in an evangelical church. I had an adolescent case of impostor syndrome that I could never really shake. For instance, even though I participated in church activities more frequently than almost anyone my age, I didn't get baptized until I was fifteen years old. In comparison, many of my Sunday school peers made that decision in elementary school, during Vacation Bible School. I just couldn't convince myself to be sure of any of it. When the pastor would declare with a raised voice and clenched jaw, "Jesus is the only way to heaven," my immediate reaction was "How can you be so sure?" I was always jealous of people who just knew Christianity to be true.

Mainline sermons, in contrast, would often contain phrases like "I think what this passage of Scripture means . . ." or "There are several ways scholars have interpreted this parable of Jesus." I appreciated the intellectual exercise that was necessary to engage with a sermon that posed a series of complex questions rather than a list of simple answers.

However, after becoming enamored with the mainline's approach to the Bible, theology, and truth, I quickly faced a stark reality: The mainline was dying, and rapidly.

Challenging Mainline Misconceptions

I have been on staff at three American Baptist churches. Two of them have ceased to exist; the third is significantly smaller today than it was two decades ago and is likely headed toward dissolution. In the American Baptist denomination, very few churches are avoiding rapid decline, which means very few churches can support full-time ministers. There just aren't enough people in the pews to justify the expense. Finding a bivocational pastor can be a real challenge for many congregations in more rural regions, making it even more difficult for those houses of worship to keep their doors open.

The image many people have of the mainline is that it's full of rainbow-flag-waving, NPR-listening political progressives. As I will show you in upcoming graphs, however, survey data shows that has never really been the case. Of course, the leadership in many mainline denominations has publicly aligned with liberal causes. Yet rank-and-file members comprise an incredible mix of left, right, and center. That aggregates out to churches that are mixed political spaces.

The mainline Protestant church is emblematic of a larger phenomenon in American society: There is no place for moderates. Politicians who try to take a middle-of-the-road approach—for instance, former Senator Joe Manchin, the Democrat-turned-independent from West Virginia, or Mitt Romney, the Republican former senator from Utah—run into dead ends. Both decided not to seek reelection in 2024, knowing that doing so would likely end with their defeats by more extreme candidates.

There's a parallel story here of defeat for the mainline church: By trying to reject the extremes of evangelical Christianity on the

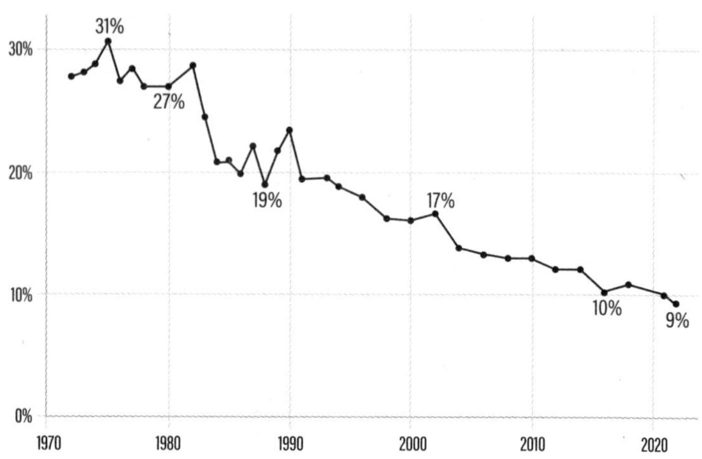

Figure 3.1 Share of the population that is mainline Protestant, 1972–2022

one hand while also resisting the pull toward nonreligion on the other, the mainline has found a way to accelerate its own demise.

According to James Hudnut-Beumler's data analysis, in the late 1950s, more than half of all Americans were associated with mainline churches. When the General Social Survey began asking questions of Americans in the early 1970s, about 30 percent of respondents aligned with mainline denominations like the United Methodist Church, the United Church of Christ, or the Episcopal Church. That figure stayed relatively high through the 1970s and into the early 1980s. But as we see in figure 3.1, the next eight years would signal a stunning decline for the mainline.

In 1982, 29 percent of Americans were mainline Protestant. Less than a decade later, that share had dropped a full ten percentage points. The mainline lost a third of its members during the Reagan years. Recall from the previous chapter that this was also the time when evangelical affiliation surged in the United States, rising about six percentage points during this span. Religious demography is a zero-sum game—if one group gets larger, another group has to get smaller. This was likely the case in the 1980s:

As the Christian right began to surge in power and prominence, many mainline Protestants defected to the evangelical tradition.

What follows this period of rapid decline is several decades of slow and steady drops. By the early 2000s, about 17 percent of Americans were mainline Protestant. But in subsequent surveys, that number dropped a percentage point or two each year. On its own, a decline of 1 percent is nothing to worry about and could be nothing more than statistical noise. But when those drops persist over the course of a decade, they signal something much more problematic. By 2016, the mainline had declined to 10 percent, and it hung around there for the next few years. In 2022, the General Social Survey reported that just 9 percent of respondents were aligned with a mainline denomination. It's stunning to consider that in the span of the average boomer's lifetime, the mainline went from half of all Americans to less than one in ten.

The United Methodist Church (UMC) may stand as the most compelling portrait of the forces shaping mainline Protestant Christianity. In the late 1960s, the UMC boasted about eleven million members. It was nearly the same size as the Southern Baptist Convention and much more geographically dispersed. The US Religion Census at that time found a United Methodist congregation in 95 percent of all counties in the United States.[2]

From that point forward, for the next fifty years, the denomination went through a slow, measured decline. It dropped below ten million by 1975 and three decades later was less than eight million. And in just the last few years, the United Methodist Church experienced one of the largest denominational schisms in American history over several theological issues, the most prominent being same-sex marriage. Between 2019 and 2023, about a quarter of all United Methodist churches chose to leave the denomination, taking about the same share of members with them. This led to a reported membership of the United Methodist Church that was less than five million in 2023—a decline of nearly 40 percent since 2006.

In total, the Seven Sisters—the seven denominations that compose the vast majority of the mainline—reported a membership of just north of twenty-four million in 1987 (see fig. 3.2). In 2022, the figure was just 13.2 million—a decline of 45 percent over the previous thirty-five years. If the number of members of the mainline had merely kept up with the overall population growth of the country, there would be around thirty-four million members today. Instead, the denomination is about a third that size. By any metric, the religious group that has taken the hardest hit over the last several decades is mainline Protestant Christianity.

And there's little reason to believe that the declines will slow down. According to their own records, half of the members of the Episcopal Church have celebrated their sixty-fifth birthday, while just 13 percent of members are under the age of eighteen. From 2017 onward, Episcopal priests have conducted more burials than baptisms. Among the members of the Presbyterian Church (USA), one-third are at least seventy years old, while just 4 percent are between the ages of birth and seventeen. For an organization to merely maintain its membership numbers, it needs to offset every

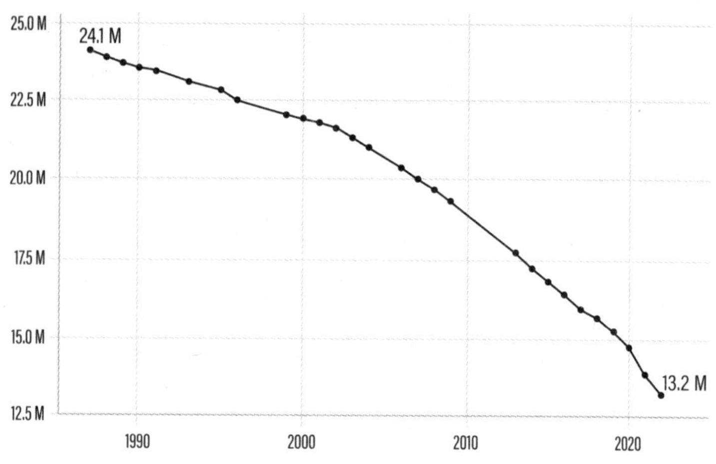

Figure 3.2 Total membership of the Seven Sisters, 1987–2022

burial with a new member joining. That's clearly not happening in most of the mainline at this point.

This statistical reality also clearly comes through when looking at survey data (see fig. 3.3). The share of the sample of the General Social Survey that were mainline Protestants between the ages of eighteen and forty in the 1970s was at least 10 percent. But as the total share of the population that is mainline has declined, so has the share who are younger adults. Just about 2 percent of all respondents to the 2022 General Social Survey were adult members of mainline Protestant churches and were no older than forty. The long-term implications of this are simple: There are very few mainline Protestants in their prime childbearing years. That means the number of baptisms and confirmations will continue to drop. At the same time, if a young professional decides to visit a mainline Protestant church in their community, they will likely be surrounded by a congregation that looks more like their grandparents than their contemporaries. That makes attracting new attendees even harder.

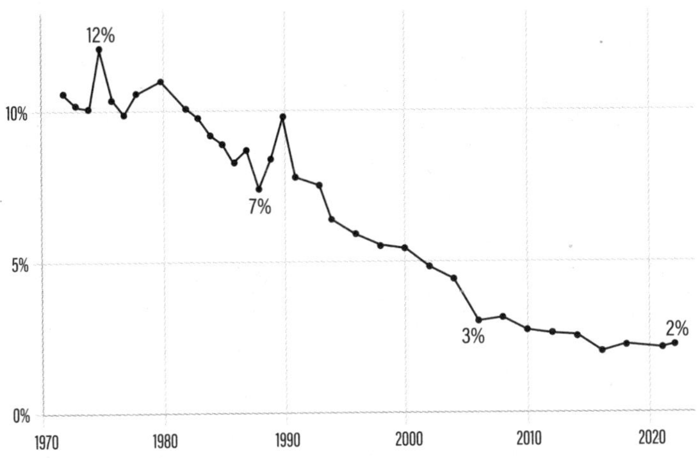

Figure 3.3 Share of the population that is mainline Protestant, ages eighteen to forty, 1972–2022

It's a vicious cycle, really. When a faith tradition sustains a long period of numerical decline, it's likely due to younger people exiting the church, not older members who have deep ties to the congregation and its history. When silver heads outnumber newborn cries in the pews, the local church has likely crossed a point of no return. Without young people, especially young couples, it's hard to maintain the same level of membership or attendance. But attracting young people to a congregation of baby boomers is an almost impossible task. Thus, it's unlikely that the mainline will see any kind of resurgence in the decades to come. What is more likely is that these denominations will have to continue to trim their budgets and capacity to carry out missionary work.

Why Strict Churches Grow

Why did the mainline suffer these tremendous losses over the last half century, though? In 1972, Dean M. Kelley offered one explanation in the book *Why Conservative Churches Are Growing*. Kelley noted a simple statistical fact: Liberal churches had sustained the largest losses in members between the 1950s and 1970s, while more conservative traditions like the Southern Baptist Convention were continuing to grow at a steady pace.[3] Kelley believed this was due to conservative churches being better at attracting very committed members who were active in aspects of church life that extended beyond Sunday morning. They did this by demanding a high degree of fidelity to church doctrine and encouraging adherence to a specific, clearly defined lifestyle.

Kelley's theory was tested by famed economist Larry Iannaccone in an important paper titled "Why Strict Churches Are Strong."[4] Iannaccone's argument is based on rational choice theory, which posits that people engage in behaviors that have more benefits than costs. Scholars who work in this field often describe humans as utility maximizers, always looking to get through life with as little costs as possible. But religion proves to be a huge problem for rational choice theory in that it's quite possible that church members may attend services, enjoy a churchwide potluck, and demand time of the pastor without dropping a dollar into the collection plate or bringing a dish to the fellowship meal. Strictness solves this problem by screening out those free riders. Iannaccone argues that the use of "penalties and prohibition" against behaviors that violate the religious group's beliefs serves as a winnowing mechanism. This effectively increases the cost of being a part of the religious group; lukewarm members quickly glean that membership is now providing negative utility. They have two choices: leave or become even more committed to the group to reduce their costs.

The mainline church tradition stands in direct opposition to the idea of strictness. Mainline churches tend to elevate concepts like openness, toleration, and diversity as opposed to narrow dogmas and uniformity. Kelley and Iannaccone would both argue that as the mainline churches have tried to be too many things to too many people, they have effectively made it incredibly easy for many members to "free ride." While evangelical churches often place a strong emphasis on regular attendance and consistent engagement with midweek Bible studies and other church activities, the same is not often the case for mainline Protestants.

Evangelicals are much more likely than mainline Protestants to attend church services nearly every week or more. Even back in the early 1970s, about 45 percent were attending nearly every week compared with only about 30 percent of mainliners. In the mid-1990s, evangelical attendance began to steadily increase, ending up around 55 percent in the most recent survey data. The mainline trend line is much less dramatic. Attendance stayed relatively close to 30 percent until it began to slowly tail off in the last few years (see fig. 3.4).

Recall that the share of Americans who were mainline Protestants dropped significantly during this period. For those who

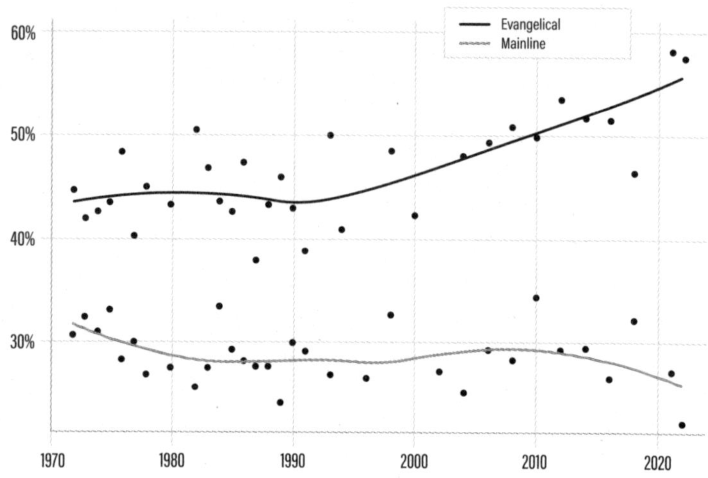

Figure 3.4 Share of mainline Protestants who attend church nearly every week or more, 1972–2022

stuck around, their devotion stayed relatively constant. However, based on this data, there's no doubt that the evangelical tradition demands a strictness and a conformity that is not found in mainline churches—it's easier to come when it's convenient and be a free rider at the local church. Evangelicalism has become more of an "all in or all out" phenomenon. This seemingly hasn't had a significant deleterious effect on its numbers, at least compared with the mainline.

It is striking to consider, though, that in the 2020 data, an evangelical Protestant was about twice as likely to be a weekly attender compared with a mainliner. This means not only that the total number of mainline Protestants is dropping considerably but also that the share of them who carry the administrative load at the local church is incredibly small. Even if we compare a mainline church to an evangelical one of a similar size, we will find that the evangelical pastor will have twice as many regular attenders to help coordinate events and engage in ministry in the community. Also, given the problem that the mainline has with the age distribution of its membership, it's quite possible that many in lay leadership roles may not be physically able to serve much longer—and there's no younger generation in place to carry the torch.

Political Diversity as Denominational Liability

Beyond lower levels of participation, political diversity may also be making it difficult for the mainline tradition to retain its members.

The political composition of the mainline Protestant church has changed very little from what it was five decades ago. In 1972, about 47 percent of mainliners were Republicans and 42 percent were Democrats, with the remainder identifying as independents. In the decades that followed, the Republican share did creep up to slightly above 50 percent, while the Democrat percentage dropped a few points. But eventually those lines began to converge again. And in the most recent data, the number of mainline Democrats and mainline Republicans is essentially one to one. Again, at the lay level, the mainline is more politically diverse than viral headlines and tweets might suggest (see fig. 3.5).

Many readers may be surprised to see that there's been no period in the last fifty years when the mainline had more Democrats than Republicans. Remember, the conception that many people have of the mainline is that it is a liberal denomination that discusses issues like LGBTQ+ rights and social justice on a regular basis. That is certainly true of the leadership in many of the most prominent denominations. In 2003, Paul Djupe and Christopher Gilbert published a book that used survey data from clergy from the Evangelical Lutheran Church in America and the Episcopal Church. They found a tremendous disconnect between the views of clergy and the views of members and attendees.[5] The clergy in those denominations tend to be much further to the left of the political spectrum than those whom they pastor. The median member of a United Methodist Church is a moderate Republican

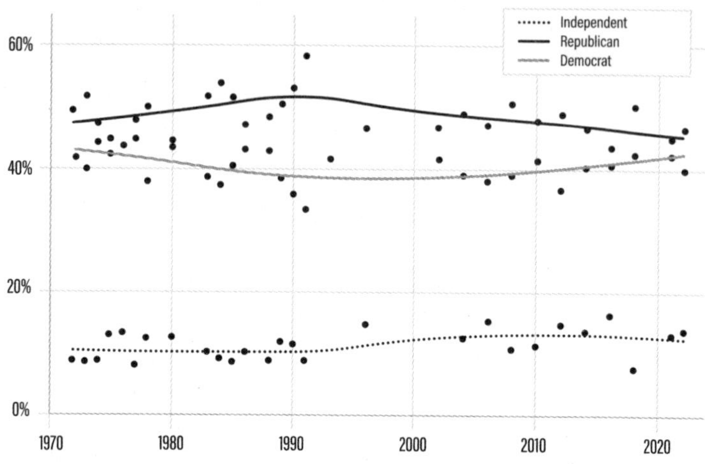

Figure 3.5 The political partisanship of mainline Protestants, 1972–2022

who tends to take a pragmatic view on issues like abortion and same-sex marriage and who favors lower taxes and less regulation. This logically follows because many mainline Protestants have earned college degrees and enjoy above-average incomes.

A simple calculation to determine the political diversity of a group is to subtract the percentage of people who identify with one party from the percentage that identifies with the other party. A score of zero indicates that there is one Democrat for every Republican in a specific group. As the number rises, it indicates an increase in political polarization—one party is clearly outnumbering the other.

As can quickly be ascertained from figure 3.6, the polarization score for mainline Protestants has been fairly low over the last fifty years. At times, the Republicans outnumbered the Democrats, but not by a wide margin. In recent years, the two percentages have largely converged. When we plot the polarization score of mainline Protestants compared with that of white evangelicals over the last fifty years, a stark picture comes into clear focus regarding how these two groups diverge on issues related to politics.

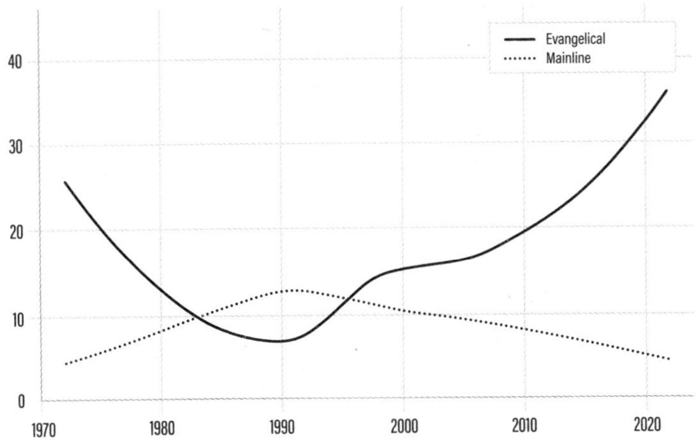

Figure 3.6 Polarization score of mainline and white evangelical Protestants, 1972–2022

In the early 1970s, the white evangelical polarization score was much higher than it was for the mainline. This was when most white evangelicals were Democrats. As many began to switch their alliance to the GOP over the following two decades, the polarization score began to drop and was lower than the score for the mainline for a period in the late 1980s into the early 1990s. But from that point forward, the trajectory of these two groups looks completely different. The score for the mainline began to move back toward zero, meaning a more even balance between Democrats and Republicans. For white evangelicals, as we covered in chapter 2, the opposite began to occur. By 2000, white evangelical Christianity was more polarized than the mainline has ever been. By 2010, the score for evangelicals was about twenty, while it was less than ten for the mainline. The latest data underscores this trend. The polarization score for the mainline was six in 2022; for the white evangelical church, it was thirty-six.

To put a fine point on this, the share of Americans who align with an evangelical tradition is the same today as it was in 1972. Among evangelicals, church attendance has never been higher. At the same time, the white evangelical church was more diverse in 1972 than it was in 2022—when 63 percent identified as Republicans and just 17 percent as Democrats. Meanwhile, the share of mainline Protestants in the population has dropped by two-thirds, from 30 percent to less than 10 percent in the most recent data. The share of mainline Protestants who attend services nearly every week is around 25 percent today, a slight drop from a decade ago and less than half the rate among evangelicals. Meanwhile, the tradition is more politically diverse today than it has been at any point since the 1970s.

Margaret Thatcher, the UK's first female prime minister, once said, "Standing in the middle of the road is very dangerous; you get knocked down by the traffic from both sides."[6] That quote seems incredibly applicable when thinking about the trajectory of mainline Protestantism. By refusing to pick a side, those in the mainline have managed to be painted as too liberal by evangelicals and too conservative by nonreligious Americans. Political diversity is not an organizational strength in twenty-first-century America, as people continue to seek out spaces that reinforce viewpoints rather than challenge assumptions. It creates a branding problem for the mainline as well. The average American likely knows what they are getting themselves into when they choose to attend an evangelical church. The same can't be said for a mainline congregation. Some of them are incredibly progressive, while others are clearly right of center on political and theological issues.

The mainline used to be the loudest and most influential voice in American Protestant Christianity. Now, that voice has largely been silenced. Striving for a tradition that welcomes all viewpoints and political proclivities may represent a deeply held conviction for many proud members of the mainline, but it has not proven to be a viable pathway for organizational vitality. As the American political landscape has continued to sort into very conservative Republicans and incredibly progressive Democrats, those who choose to stand between the two extremes are often in very small company. In his poem "The Second Coming," William Butler Yeats writes, "Things fall apart; the centre cannot hold."[7] That's certainly become the case in white American Christianity.

This political sorting, of course, extends outside the four walls of the local Methodist or Episcopal church, however. Houses of worship are places where people feel more socially disarmed among other members of the group. They are willing to listen to opposing arguments and seriously consider new ways of thinking about the Bible, their community, and the larger democracy. Mainline churches used to be ideal places to tamp down tensions, not inflame divisions. But the number of institutions in American life that are made up of politically and socially diverse people has dwindled. The great calming effect that churches can have has been severely limited. Now, people on the far left and the far right can hurl epithets at one another while safely behind their keyboards, knowing full well that they will never meet their online opponent in a very real pew on Sunday morning.

Facing the humanity of another human being can be incredibly effective at turning down the rhetoric and turning up the compassion and openness. Where I live, the local United Methodist church has one of the largest food pantries and clothes closets in the entire community. When I go to help, I see volunteers who come from every part of the political spectrum, and I know that some of them are proudly secular. But all these people with disparate voices and viewpoints work together to meet the common objective of community service. And in the process, they build bridges of compassion not just between those volunteering and those being served but also among those who choose to give up a few hours on a weekday morning to help others in need—regardless of their political or religious opinions. When mainline churches close, opportunities to serve the less fortunate and build social capital will largely be lost.

4

American Catholics

THE BIG TAKEAWAYS

- The Catholic Church is the largest religious institution in the United States, managing to resist schisms despite its growing diversity.
- However, the future of white Catholicism is increasingly conservative, with priests and parishioners alike moving further to the right.

There is no religious organization in the United States like the Roman Catholic Church. According to the most recent data, there are sixty-two million members of the Catholic Church. In comparison, the largest Protestant denomination, the Southern Baptist Convention, has a membership of thirteen million. In other words, there are nearly five Catholics for every Southern Baptist in the United States. While many denominations have a geographical concentration—Southern Baptists in the Bible Belt, Evangelical Lutherans in the northern plains—Catholic churches can be found nearly everywhere. The Religion Census managed to find a Catholic house of worship in 94 percent of all US counties.[1]

Catholicism is part of the conversation in big cities, rural areas, and everywhere in between.

Even a casual look at American Protestant Christianity reveals a common refrain: schism. It's hard to find a major denominational family that hasn't splintered into several factions. There are Southern, American, and Free Will Baptists along with dozens of other smaller organizations just in that one faith tradition. There are Evangelical Lutherans and Lutherans from the Missouri Synod, each with over a million members. That's just not the case with the Catholic Church. While there are a small number of independent Catholic denominations, the Roman Catholic Church is almost completely unified in the United States and recognizes the pope as its head.

The fact that one can visit a Catholic church in Seattle, Washington, and rural Pennsylvania, finding both to be part of the same organization and following roughly the same order of service, is staggering considering the cultural and political differences between those two parts of the country. While the trend in Protestant Christianity over the last several decades has been not only to leave denominations but also to launch thousands of nondenominational churches, Catholicism has withstood the urge to divide and purify more than any large religious organization in the United States.

That said, the Catholic Church in the US may not be able to resist the fragmentation and division that have become so deeply ingrained in American society over the last several years. And this means that a faith tradition that is orders of magnitude larger than any Protestant denomination and is found in every region of the United States will no longer be a unifying force in American society and democracy. Instead of trying to bridge the racial divide and the growing chasm between urban and rural America, it will instead be just one more echo chamber in the lives of the faithful—reinforcing their worst fears about the other side of the political aisle.

A growing number of very conservative Catholics are seeking to push the church to the right on theological and social issues. In the last several years, "traditional Catholics"—or "trad Caths"—have been raising their voices. They believe that the church is heading in the wrong direction and that there needs to be a concerted effort to return to a more conservative Catholicism, especially in the United States. Given that there are over sixty million Catholics in the United States, it would stand to reason that there's always been a contingent that believes that the church is experiencing a liberal drift. However, social media has made it easier for trad Catholics to find one another and spread their message to the larger church with once-impossible ease and immediacy.

When an organization (religious or not) is experiencing consistent growth, it's harder for reformers to get a foothold to discuss ways to make things better. To employ an overused sports adage, "Winning solves everything." Even when there are clear weaknesses in a religious tradition, they are easy to ignore when membership is growing or even relatively stable. That has certainly been the case in the Catholic Church over the last fifty years (see fig. 4.1).

In the 1970s, the share of the sample that was Catholic in the General Social Survey was between 25 and 28 percent. Over the

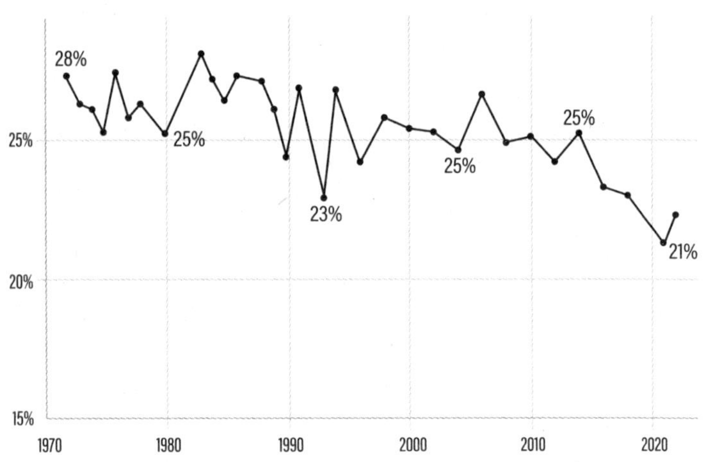

Figure 4.1 Share of the population that is Catholic, 1972–2022

next several decades, the number consistently settled at about 25 percent. In 1980, 25 percent of the sample was Catholic. Thirty-four years later, in 2014, it was the same percentage. Given how volatile American religion was during that period, this consistency is remarkable. Yet 2014 was the last time that the Catholic percentage would be so high. In the last several waves of the survey, the percentage eroded. It was 23 percent in 2016 and 2018, dropped to 21 percent in 2021, and then rebounded just slightly to 22 percent in 2022. It's fair to say that there's been a small (probably three-percentage-point) drop in the Catholic share in the last eight years.

A Racially Diverse Body

Scholars of American religion often analyze Protestant Christianity based, in no small part, on race. For instance, mainline Christians are overwhelmingly white. While groups like the United Methodist Church have tried to diversify by investing vast amounts of resources in places like Africa, the denomination is nearly 90 percent white in the United States. Additionally, there's a vast network of historically Black churches like the African Methodist Episcopal Church and the National Baptist Convention. It's rare to find a Protestant church or even a denomination that has a racial diversity that matches the overall composition of the United States. The Catholic Church can't spin off a new denomination to cater to Asian Americans in California or the growing number of Hispanics in places like Texas or Arizona. Instead, it has to find ways to accommodate the country's growing diversity.

The data indicates that the only reason the Catholic Church has not declined more rapidly is because it has drawn a large number of nonwhite members (see fig. 4.2). In 1972, about 95 percent of all Catholics in the General Social Survey identified as white. However, as time passed, the white share of the Catholic Church began to decline and the pews started including more Hispanic, Asian, and African American adherents. Between 1972

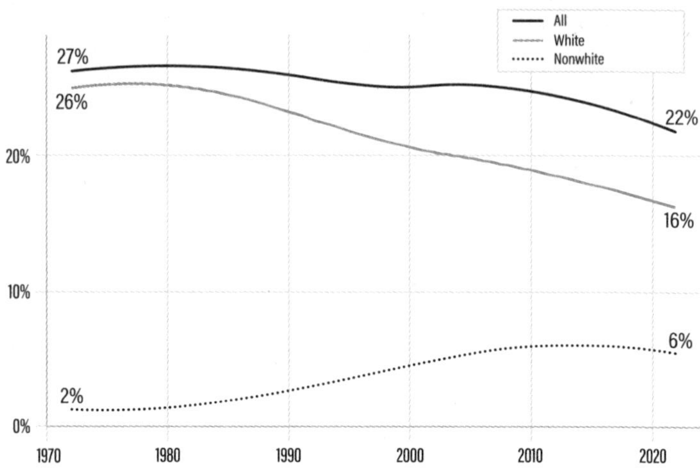

Figure 4.2 Share of the population that is Catholic divided into white and nonwhite categories, 1972–2022

and 2022, the share of all adults in the United States who were white Catholics declined from 26 to 16 percent. At the same time, the share of nonwhite Catholics rose from 1.6 to 6 percent. Now, white Catholics are only 73 percent of the church's membership.

From a purely sociological point of view, it's much easier for an organization to be unified when there is little racial diversity. Priests face logistical challenges when trying to serve a growing number of Hispanic members who would prefer a Mass in Spanish, especially in a church that has been overwhelmingly white in its American permutation for decades. It's also important to note that race is one of the primary cleavages in the American political landscape. White Christians are overwhelmingly politically conservative and vote in large numbers for Republican candidates. It's much more a mixed bag with nonwhite Christians. In prior decades, that would not have been a difficult issue to navigate. But when politics seems to be in the background of every discussion, a request to add a Mass for non-English speakers can have ideological undertones. Some more conservative members of the local parish may believe that the role of the church should be to assimilate immigrants into American society, not segregate them further by offering Mass in Spanish.

What exacerbates the numerical decline of Catholics over the last fifty years is something that may be even more damaging to the church: the absolute collapse in Mass attendance since the early 1970s. Recall that in 1972 about 28 percent of all American adults identified as Catholic. More remarkably, the average Catholic was fairly active in their local parish. Nearly half reported attending Mass almost every week or more. The proportion of Catholics who said that they never attended Mass was just 12 percent. Thus, nearly all Catholics were attending Mass at least once a year, and a sizable portion were attending services on a regular basis (see fig. 4.3).

The data makes clear that the early 1970s was the golden age of American Catholicism. From that point on, weekly Mass attendance dropped, dipping below 40 percent by 1990 and below 30 percent by 2010. In the most recent survey conducted in 2022, just 23 percent of all Catholics said that they attend Mass almost

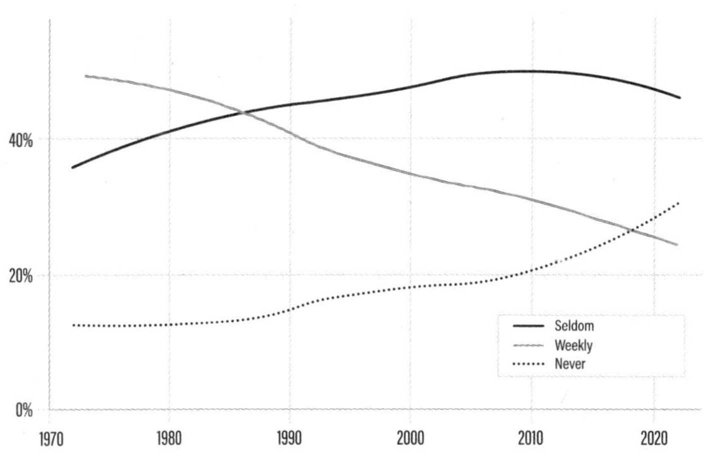

Figure 4.3 Mass attendance among Catholics, 1972–2022

every week or more. That's half the rate it was five decades earlier. Meanwhile, the share of never-attending Catholics crept up slowly for several decades. It took about forty years for the never-attending share to rise from 12 to 20 percent. But in just twelve years, between 2010 and 2022, that share rose an additional ten percentage points. Now, there are more US Catholics who never attend Mass than there are Catholics who attend nearly every week or more.

It's helpful to think about this decline in terms of larger percentages as well. For instance, in 1972, 13.5 percent of all American adults were Catholics who attended Mass every week or more. In 2022, the share of the adult population that fit those criteria was just 5.5 percent. In raw numbers, about 30 million Americans were regularly attending Catholics in 1972. Today, that number is closer to 18 million. Meanwhile, 22.5 million people self-identify as Catholic but report that they never attend Mass. There is no doubt that the Catholic Church is significantly smaller today than it was during the 1970s, and there's little reason to believe that this trend will reverse in the near future given the data in figure 4.4.

It's remarkable how straight these lines are for each generation over a period of decades. For instance, the silent generation (those born between 1925 and 1945) changed very little between 1972 and 2012. About half of silent generation Catholics were in Mass weekly. The number began to drop only as that generation became less physically able to make it to church every week. Boomers did experience some decline during their lifetime, but it was gradual. About 40 percent of them were weekly attenders in the early 1970s. Today, that number is about 30 percent, but no single period revealed a rapid decline.

Generation X and millennials are more intriguing. When they entered adulthood, a little more than 20 percent of Gen X Catholics were regular attenders, and it's basically the same share today. For millennials, Mass attendance was never that high. It started at around 18 percent when the oldest millennials became adults, and

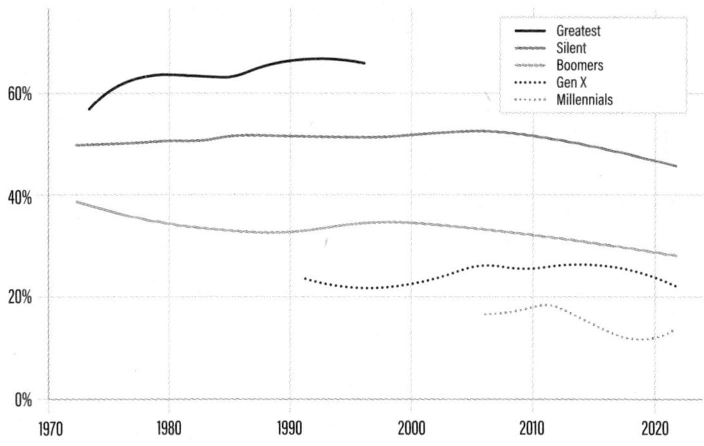

Figure 4.4 Share of Catholics who attend Mass nearly every week or more by generation, 1972–2022

now it's closer to 16 percent. But, again, that's not a noticeable drop over a period of fifteen years.

So if all these lines are running nearly straight, why has overall Mass attendance declined? Because every successive generation is a bit less active in their faith than the prior one. Boomers were about ten points less likely to attend than members of the silent generation, and Gen Xers were about ten points lower than the boomers. The gap between millennials and Gen Xers is smaller (only about five points), but most likely that's because the overall percentage of attendees is coming closer to zero.

What looms large in the background of any discussion of declining Mass attendance is the Catholic Church's sexual abuse scandal and the vast attempt by church leaders to cover up the truth when they became aware of the allegations. Many people will look at these graphs pertaining to Catholic Mass attendance and conclude that this was a turning point in the trajectory of American Catholicism. However, the data doesn't tell such a clear story. *The Boston Globe*'s Spotlight Team didn't publish its first report of the abuse until early 2002. Weekly Mass attendance had already dropped by fifteen percentage points before the public was aware of the allegations. In the two decades since the abuse allegations became public, weekly Mass attendance dropped from 35 to 25 percent. While it may seem logical to conclude that the fallout from the abuse scandal drove Catholics from the pews, the data says that they were already abandoning the church in droves long before *The Boston Globe* broke the story.

The Politics of Modern Catholicism

Politics, of course, may be (partly) to blame for Catholic decline over the last several decades. To be sure, it's hard to easily describe the political climate of the Catholic Church over the last fifty years. A Catholic church in New England is going to be different from one in the suburbs of Phoenix. Some dioceses are overwhelmingly white, and others are incredibly racially diverse. Urban Catholics think about politics differently than those who live in sparsely populated parts of the country's midsection. Even so, the data does point toward some consistent trends in the overall political trajectory of Catholicism.

First, let's look at the political identity of white Catholics over the last fifty years (see fig. 4.5).

The election of John F. Kennedy in 1960 as the country's first Catholic president may serve as a benchmark for measuring white Catholics' political partisanship. White working-class Catholic Democrats in the Northeast were one of his most valuable voting blocs. Even into the 1970s, the data indicates that white Catholics were overwhelmingly Democrat. However, by the late 1980s, the Democratic Party was losing some of its advantage with white Catholics. What's fascinating is how very little changed regarding the partisan composition of white Catholics between the mid-1990s into the early 2010s.

Then, for the first time in the modern era, around Donald Trump's presidential victory in 2016, the percentage of white Catholic Republicans began to surpass those who aligned with the

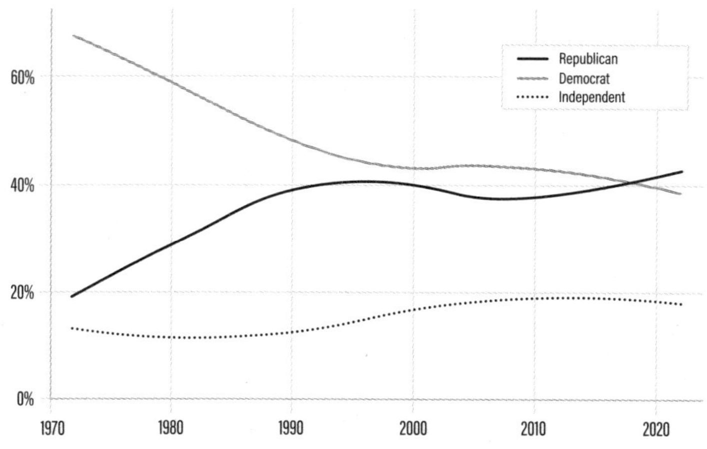

Figure 4.5 The political partisanship of white Catholics, 1972–2022

Democrats, and trend lines are pointing to the Republican share accelerating over time. According to the 2024 Cooperative Election Study, 64 percent of white Catholics voted for Donald Trump in his 2024 campaign against Kamala Harris. That was an eight percentage point increase from John McCain's result in 2008.[2]

For decades, white Catholicism was politically heterogeneous. A Democrat may have taken Communion right after a Republican during Sunday Mass. That is becoming less and less the case now—in white churches at least.

What makes this lack of heterogeneity particularly worrisome is that in many smaller towns the Catholic Church has just one parish. In contrast, a town of twenty-five thousand residents may have fifty or sixty Protestant churches. That means, quite simply, that the local Catholic Mass may be the largest gathering of people in a community on a given week. As previously discussed, many Protestant denominations often have an implied socioeconomic and racial component. Given the singular nature of the Catholic Church, this has never been the case for the local parish. It's made up of rich and poor, white people and people of color. From a purely social scientific perspective, nothing compares to the gathering for weekend Mass in many parts of the United States. It may be the only opportunity that exists for people from diverse backgrounds to meet in a social space on a regular basis. However, with the political sorting happening among white Catholics, this space is transitioning from a place of tremendous diversity to a place that is less and less welcoming to those who find themselves on the left side of the political spectrum.

The story for nonwhite Catholics is much different—and harder to describe. What complicates matters is that there just weren't that many nonwhite Catholics in samples of the general population for decades. Even through the 1990s, less than 5 percent of all American adults identified as nonwhite Catholics. Given that limitation, the partisan trend lines for nonwhite Catholics look much different from those for their white counterparts.

If there's one consistent finding in the data, it's that a majority of nonwhite Catholics have been Democrats for the last fifty years. In the 1970s, the Democratic share was about 60 percent. That has

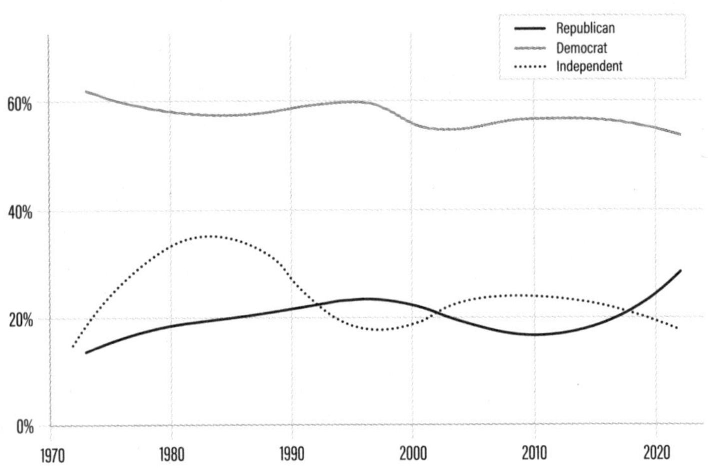

Figure 4.6 The political partisanship of nonwhite Catholics who attend Mass nearly every week, 1972–2022

eroded a bit over time, but even in the most recent data collected, 55 percent of nonwhite Catholics said that they were Democrats. The Republican share has vacillated a bit but until recently has stayed close to about 20 percent of nonwhite Catholics.

That said, there's been a clear uptick in the share of Republican nonwhite Catholics. In 2022, just 30 percent of nonwhite Catholics told pollsters that they were Republicans, but according to the Cooperative Election Study, 40 percent of nonwhite Catholics were Trump voters in 2024, compared to only 24 percent when Trump ran for president in 2016.[3] Additionally, I conducted a county-level analysis of voting results in 2024 compared with 2020 and found that places that moved the most significantly toward the GOP had two things in common: The largest religious tradition was Catholicism, and huge portions of the population were Hispanic. So it may very well be the case that Latino Catholics will move in the direction of the Republican Party in future elections.

There are other indicators that the Catholic Church is beginning to swing solidly to the right. If one wants to chart the direction of a religious tradition, it's helpful to look at the youngest adult members, especially those who are the most actively involved in their local churches. While the Catholic Church has a strong hierarchy, no organization is immune to the opinions of those who fill the pews each Sunday. If the sample is divided into generations and then weekly-attending white Catholics are compared with all white respondents, it becomes much easier to chart the course of American Catholicism. Look at figure 4.7 to see how each generation of white Catholics aligns politically.

Among older white Catholics who attend Mass every week, a strong majority are Republicans. Also note how little distance there is between these active white Catholics and white members of their generation as a whole. For instance, there's only a five-point gap in Republican share among the silent generation. It's nine points among baby boomers. The gap widens between active white Generation X Catholics and the rest of their birth cohort. About

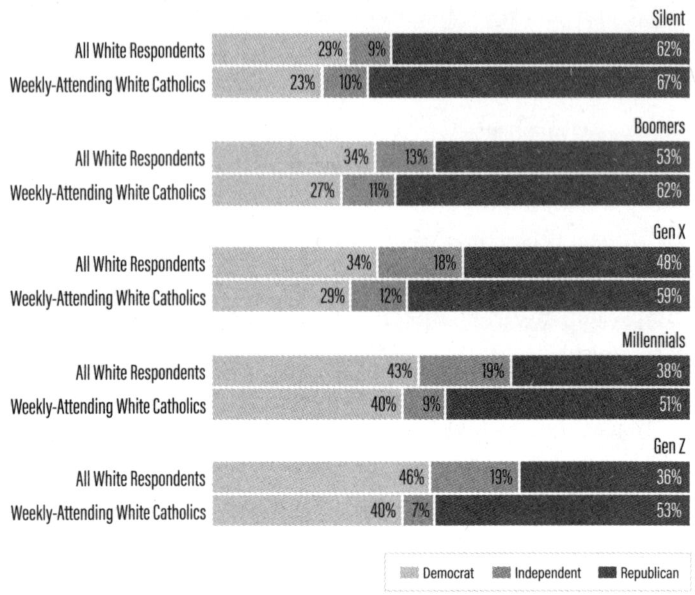

Figure 4.7 The political partisanship of weekly-attending white Catholics by generation, 2020–23

59 percent of active white Catholics are Republicans, compared with just 48 percent of white members of Generation X as a whole.

That gulf only continues to widen when comparing millennials and Generation Z active white Catholics with their generations as a whole. Among white millennial Catholics who attend Mass weekly, a majority are Republicans—51 percent. Among white millennials as a whole, just 38 percent identify as Republicans. For Gen Z, the gap is even larger. Among those young adults who attend Mass regularly, 53 percent say they are Republicans, a larger share than found among the active millennial Catholics. Among white Gen Z members as a whole, only 36 percent are Republicans. It's apparent from this angle that young people who self-identify as being active Catholics are much different from other members of their generation. Among millennials and Gen Z, Catholic identity is coded Republican.

This widening political distance between young white Catholics and the rest of their generation portends a number of sociological issues facing the country in the future.

First, the Catholic Church is becoming increasingly linked with conservative politics. Thus, a young person who is moderate or left of center may not even consider becoming active in a local congregation. Second, when this distance increases, it becomes apparent that young people are self-selecting into Catholic parishes because, in part, they want to surround themselves with people who have a posture toward politics and theology similar to their own. Third and finally, it is likely that American society will bifurcate based on this growing divide. In other words, nonchurchgoers will have little interaction with those who are incredibly active in their faith. As we will explore later, this may be the most troublesome part of this growing trend.

Young people sorting themselves into religious and conservative or nonreligious and liberal will make it even more difficult to navigate some of the most troubling challenges facing the United States going forward. Imagine young people trying to have a debate on college campuses about the ability of a woman to obtain an abortion when half the class is made up of conservative Catholics and evangelicals and the other half is made up of very progressive, secular students. Without moderate and progressive people of faith, and without at least some conservative atheists, common ground becomes nearly impossible. Or what happens in a local high school that's trying to navigate issues related to students who identify as transgender? One part of the student body will push the administration to not recognize nonbinary young people, while the other part will seek to find as many accommodations as are allowed under the law. In the middle of that ideological chasm is a young person just trying to make sense of their gender identity, not become some type of political talking point.

The Growing Conservative Priesthood

In 2022, researchers from the Catholic University of America sent surveys to ten thousand priests. The questionnaire touched on a variety of topics related to politics, culture, and the demographics of each respondent. The results, based on 3,516 respondents, offer tremendous insight into the overall composition of the priesthood and what the new crop of priests looks like today in terms of theology and political views (see fig. 4.8).

Priests were asked to describe their theological views with response options that ranged from "very progressive" to "very conservative." They could also choose "middle of the road." The data becomes incredibly telling when broken down by the decade in which priests were ordained. For instance, among those who were ordained in the late 1960s, the vast majority (68 percent) said that their theology was progressive. The remaining portions were evenly split between the middle of the road and conservative options.

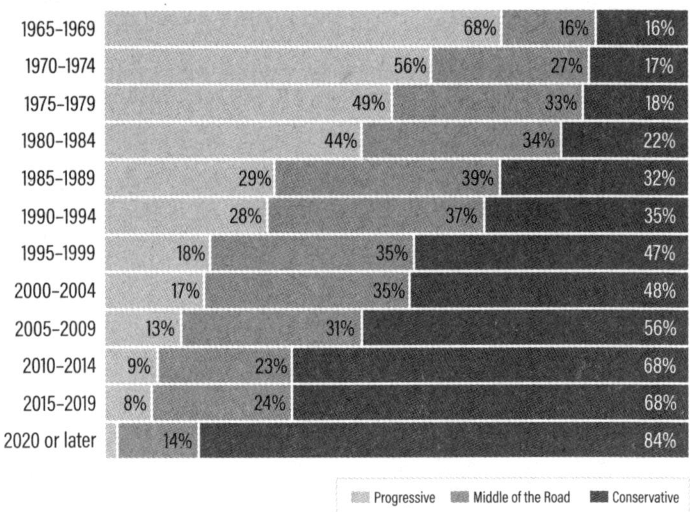

Figure 4.8 Self-described theological views of priests by decade of ordination, 2022

With each successive ordination cohort, priests began to shift decidedly to the right. For instance, among priests who received ordination between 1980 and 1984, 44 percent called themselves progressive, while those in the middle of the road jumped to 34 percent. Just one cohort later, the balance shifted even more. Among those ordained in the late 1980s and early 1990s, the distribution between progressive and conservative was close to equal, while the largest share said that they were middle of the road.

This delicate balance would be over by the late 1990s. Among priests who were ordained between 1995 and 1999, 47 percent said that they were conservative and only 18 percent said that they were progressive. Just ten years later, the conservative share jumped to 56 percent, while the progressive percentage dropped to just 13 percent. By 2010, the number of progressive priests being ordained was less than 10 percent. Among those who were ordained as priests in the last five years, just 2 percent said that they were progressive, while 84 percent were conservative. In addition, the share of priests who describe themselves as middle of the road is the smallest it's ever been. The Catholic priesthood in the United States will likely be almost completely theologically homogeneous in the next thirty years as older priests retire and are replaced by new priests who are uniformly conservative.

It's not just theology where priests are more conservative. In 2020, the Austin Institute surveyed just over a thousand Catholic priests about matters of theology and political ideology. Again, breaking down the data by ordination year is instructive (see fig. 4.9). Among priests who were ordained before 1981, there was a nice mix of political views: 38 percent were progressive, 38 percent were middle of the road, and 24 percent were conservative. However, that balanced distribution didn't last long. In the next decade of ordination, the middle-of-the-road share didn't change. It remained at 38 percent. However, the progressive share dropped twenty points, and the conservative percentage rose by the same amount.

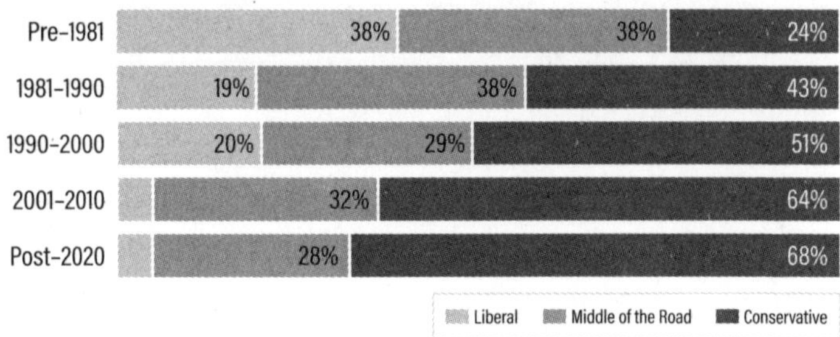

Figure 4.9 Self-described political views of priests by decade of ordination, 2020

By the 1990s, the priesthood had a rightward tilt—one that has gotten steeper ever since. Among priests born in the first decade of the 2000s, 64 percent were conservative and just 4 percent were progressive. Among the most newly ordained, 68 percent were conservative and 2 percent were politically progressive.

Let's be clear. The issue here is not that conservatives are dominating the ranks of incoming priests. It is that the priesthood is now largely a monolith in both theology and political ideology. Imagine a young person who starts reading the writings of the Catholic social activist Dorothy Day, a woman who was motivated by her faith to embrace a life of voluntary poverty and champion workers' rights and social justice. Attending a service at the local parish would likely be jarring, as Day's ideals would not be espoused by the priest during the homily. Even if a town has multiple Catholic parishes, it's unlikely that any of them will be led by a true left-of-center priest in the next few decades.

There's another ramification of this increasing shift to the right among Catholic priests: They seem incredibly dissatisfied with the current state of the church (see fig. 4.10). Few among the thousand or so survey respondents believed that the Catholic Church was "excellent." But looking at the type of priest who rated the church as "good" is incredibly instructive. This type described their personal politics as moderate. The priests least likely to say that the church is good were very liberal (12 percent) or very conservative

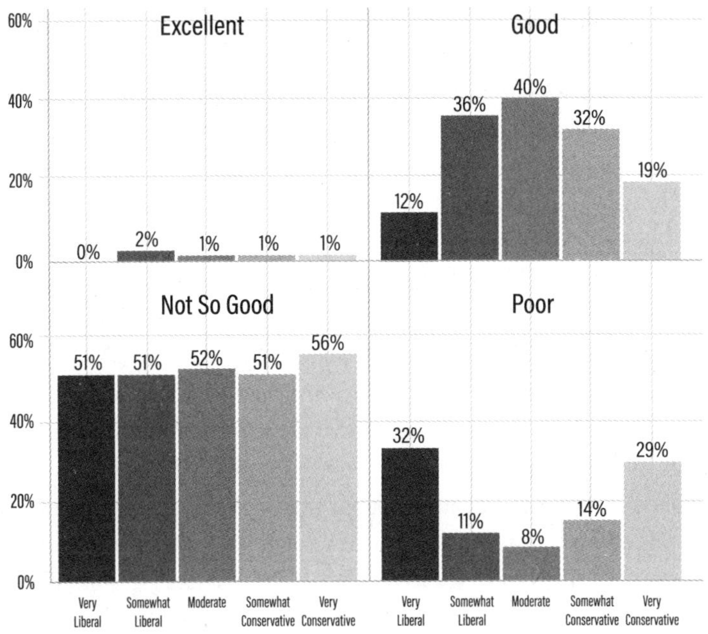

Figure 4.10 Self-described views of the Catholic Church among priests based on their personal politics, 2020

(19 percent). Those on the ends of the spectrum had a more negative perspective than those in the middle.

That growing polarization and its consequences comes into sharper focus when looking at the types of priests who rated the church as "poor." Just 8 percent of moderates believed that the church was in poor shape—the lowest of any category. Among very liberal priests, 32 percent said that the church was in poor shape in the United States. Meanwhile, a similar proportion of very conservative priests (29 percent) chose the "poor" option. In other words, the priests on both ends of the political spectrum were the least satisfied with the current state of the church, while the moderates seemed reasonably pleased.

I don't think it takes much guesswork to figure out what is happening here. Very liberal priests were unhappy because the church was too conservative. Very conservative priests offered negative assessments because the church was not far enough to the right.

This may be the most searing indictment for the state of the Catholic Church—and Christianity as a whole—in the United States. People on the ends of the political spectrum want their religious tradition to reflect their own political proclivities. When it doesn't, they believe it means the church is in a state of disarray. It's possible that moderates were relatively pleased with the state of things because they saw a church that was ideologically divided and found some comfort in the fact that both conservatives and liberals were filling the pews. The moderate Catholic priest (and likely the moderate Catholic) does not want to see a church that is split in two by political factions. The beauty and the brilliance of the Catholic faith, not just in the United States but globally, is that it has actively resisted splintering. Even though the church has a significant presence in every corner of the planet, has tremendous racial diversity, and has members from every part of the ideological spectrum, it is still the universal church.

Think about the spiritual (and sociological) power that comes from the feeling of taking part in a Mass in South Philadelphia that is basically the same as a Mass in South Sudan or South Korea. The Communion elements being consecrated the same way and taken in the same reverent manner by hundreds of millions of Catholics around the world is a powerful reminder of what binds people together, not what pushes them apart. That's good not just for the spiritual health of the church but for the social health of a whole society.

The data points to a future clash inside American Catholicism. The priesthood is almost completely conservative now, by any metric. Meanwhile, Catholics in the pews (especially young white Catholics) are to the right of center but not to the same extent as the priests who are finishing seminary. Also, what about dioceses with large numbers of Hispanic Catholics, or churches located in urban areas where parishioners tend to favor Democrats on Election Day? Will there be priests who can find common ground with their parishioners?

The rise of the traditional Catholic may also signal a growing fracture in the American Catholic Church. During the Second Vatican Council, church leadership made a number of changes to the Mass. One was that the Mass could be conducted in the congregation's language instead of the traditional Latin. In addition, several elements of the Mass could be omitted going forward, reducing the total time of the service significantly. American churches could have a Mass in English that often took about an hour to complete. Making the worship service more accessible was thought to be a way to draw more people into the church. Yet as previously mentioned, Mass attendance has fallen precipitously since Vatican II. Trad Caths have pointed to this in their push to return to the traditional Latin Mass. Pope Francis moved to restrict the use of the Latin Mass in 2021. In justifying his decision, he argued that the goal of the Latin Mass advocates was to divide Catholicism and oppose church reforms, not to bring a new crop of converts into Catholicism.

According to an online directory, there are nearly five hundred sites that offer the Latin Mass to Catholics who want to return to the old ways.[4] *The New York Times* reported on this phenomenon in 2022. Ruth Graham wrote that the Latin Mass "appeals to an overlapping mix of aesthetic traditionalists, young families, new converts and critics of Pope Francis. And its resurgence, boosted by the pandemic years, is part of a rising right-wing strain within American Christianity as a whole."[5] Traditional Catholics are known for having large families, being incredibly devoted to their church, and being vocal in online circles about the value of their lifestyle and the necessity of the church to embrace their approach. Anecdotal accounts of churches that hold these Masses report tremendous growth and vitality, while attendance continues to wane with each passing year for the Mass in English.

While the push to include the Latin Mass has intensified in recent years, several bishops have made it clear where they stand on political issues. For instance, the Archbishop of San Francisco, Salvatore Cordileone, wrote an open letter to Nancy Pelosi, the former Speaker of the House, informing her that she would not be offered Communion at her home parish due to her position on abortion.[6]

While the Catholic Church has enjoyed significant political diversity in its history, those days seem to be coming to an end. The United States Conference of Catholic Bishops has made it clear where its members stand on issues related to politics. The fact that many local bishops allow or even encourage the return of the Latin Mass was seen as a strong rebuke of Pope Francis, who was often seen as a liberalizing force in the world's largest church. It seems that Catholicism is going the way of evangelical Christianity—to the right—albeit at a slightly slower pace than its Protestant cousins. In the future, American Christianity, especially white Christianity, will be even more politically and theologically conservative than it is right now.

The American Catholic Church stands as one of the true throwbacks to an earlier time in the United States. While Protestant Christianity has divided and subdivided into factions that seek to cater to the theological proclivities of incredibly small niches of American Christianity, the Catholic Church has taken its role as the "universal church" quite seriously. It has welcomed followers who are stridently social conservatives, and has sponsored the annual March for Life, which advocates for an end to abortion in the United States. But the United States Conference of Catholic Bishops has also been a strong advocate for pro-immigration policies—receiving over one hundred million dollars from the federal government to help immigrants settle into new lives in the United States. A church that defies typical political conventions is not something that should thrive in the current political environment.

Yet it seems as though the American Catholic Church's posture of bipartisanship will be coming to an end in the years to come. When just 2 to 3 percent of priests across the United States are theological or political liberals, and 85 percent are conservatives, there will be no voices holding the leadership accountable and demanding that it tack to the center in some of the most pressing and contentious issues of the day. The once-great meeting place of the Catholic Mass will look similar to what is found in American evangelicalism—a place where like-minded people talk about like-minded topics with no input from thoughtful people on the other end of the political spectrum.

5

The Nones

THE BIG TAKEAWAYS

- The religiously unaffiliated used to be an incredibly small fraction of the American population. Now they are the largest "religious" group.
- Atheists and agnostics are overwhelmingly politically liberal and engage in a lot of the same practices of boundary maintenance employed by white evangelicals.

In 1972, a team of scholars launched a project that would become one of the most consequential developments in American social science. Recognizing that there were almost no large-scale, longitudinal surveys of the US population, they fielded what they called the General Social Survey. They focused on the highest standards of rigor, choosing to interview subjects in person and to ask very similar questions over a period of decades to allow researchers to track the trajectory of the American public on several key dimensions.

When it came to religion, the team simply asked people, "What is your religious preference?" and provided five response options—Protestant, Catholic, Jewish, some other religion, or no religion—in that first year of administration. In total, 1,608 people answered that question. Of those, just eighty-three of them said that they had no religious preference—about 5 percent of the total sample. It was a part of the population that many scholars studying religion had overlooked. In 1968, sociologist Glenn Vernon wrote, "The 'nones' are a neglected category, included in research designs so that percentages might total 100, rather than because it is a category worthy of analysis."[1] In other words, the nones were little more than an afterthought.

That has changed dramatically since the first General Social Survey. A quick scan of the recent literature suggests that the nones have gone from the neglected category to the group most studied by academics who analyze American religion. I believe there's been no more significant change in American society over the last thirty years than the rapid ascension of those who claim no religious affiliation.

The nones can be found in every segment of American demography. The nonreligious have grown across nearly every demographic category—gender, race, socioeconomic status, and age—compared to just ten or fifteen years ago. If one were to poll America's religious leaders about the number one concern they have right now, it's highly likely it would be related to the rise of the nones.

Dozens of books have been written about this phenomenon, including *The Great Dechurching*, to which I contributed as the lead researcher.[2] But attempts to describe why the nonreligious have risen so quickly may be overlooking a particularly important part of the story about the nones: The nonreligious in the United States—especially atheists and agnostics—are more left-leaning and politically homogeneous today than at any point in the last fifteen years. Not only have the nones risen; they are also experiencing the same purification pressures described in the previous chapters with regard to white Christians. Just as it's increasingly difficult to find someone who is to the left of center in a white

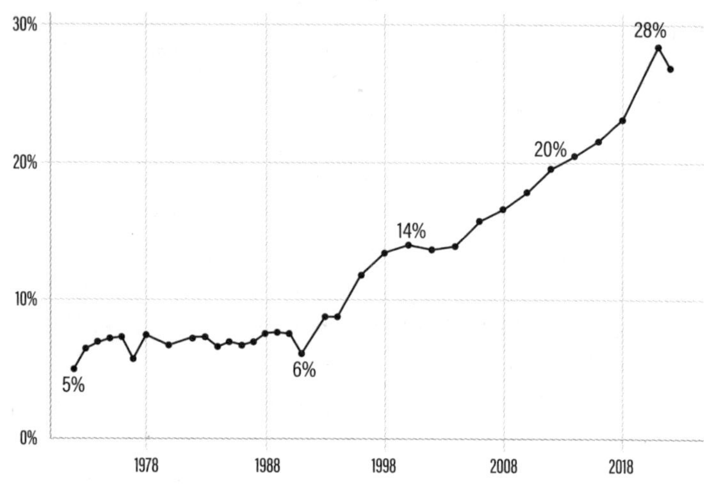

Figure 5.1 Share of the population with no religious affiliation, 1972–2022

evangelical church, it may be even more difficult to find an atheist who voted for Donald Trump or an agnostic who supports tighter restrictions on abortion. Just as conservative Christians can find ways to exclude pastors or leaders whom they believe have moved outside the bounds of orthodox theology, nonreligious groups have organizational structures and platforms that can be denied to leaders who are perceived to violate the commonly held beliefs and voting patterns of members.

Before we step into the political landscape of nonreligious Americans, it's important to assess the size, scope, and trajectory of the nones over the last several decades (see fig. 5.1).

A Group That Demands to Be Counted

As previously mentioned, the first wave of the General Social Survey (GSS) found that just 5 percent of all American adults claimed no religious affiliation. That figure was remarkably consistent through the 1970s and 1980s, but it began to edge up in the early 1990s. In 1996, the share of nones rose to double digits, more than doubling between 1991 and 1996. Their rise plateaued at 14 percent after 1998 and stayed in roughly the same spot until 2004, when the percentage began to go up again.

By 2012, the number was 20 percent, and it was 23 percent in 2018. By the time the GSS collected its 2022 results, after COVID-19 made researchers change their sampling procedures, the nones had risen to 28 percent of the population. While that number did drop by a single percentage point in the most recent survey, there's no doubt that the nones are astronomically larger now than they were just a few years ago. In fact, the nones doubled between 2004 and 2021. In real numbers, that means the share of Americans with no religious affiliation grew by at least forty million in about seventeen years.

It's worth noting that the General Social Survey provides somewhat of a blunt measure of nonreligion; it offers just one response option, "no religion." Of course, there's a vast difference between someone who proudly calls themselves an atheist and someone who just doesn't feel particularly attached to a religious tradition. Other survey instruments have tried to break down the nonreligious into more granular categories. For example, the Pew Research Center began to include several response options to a question about religious affiliation that allowed scholars to create more cohesive categories of the nonreligious. The result was a three-category typology that has been adopted by other survey instruments that want to include some questions about religion.

The share of Americans who self-described as atheists was about 3 percent of the population in 2008, and agnostics were about the same share (see fig. 5.2). What's the difference between the two groups? In the simplest terms, atheists believe there is no higher power in the universe—that there simply is no God. Thus, there is no possible mechanism for things like miracles or supernatural events to occur. Agnostics take a bit more of a measured approach to the question of a higher power. While there is certainly a variety

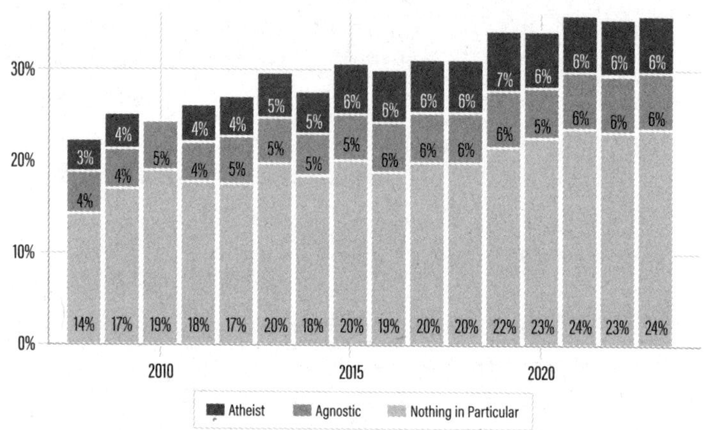

Note: The 2010 CES survey inadvertently omitted the response option for "atheist" on the questionnaire.

Figure 5.2 The rise of the nones, 2008–23

of viewpoints among agnostics, the predominant view is that there is no way to know for certain whether God exists. In other words, one cannot use science to prove (or disprove) the existence of the divine. Scholars of American religion have concluded that atheists and agnostics are united in their philosophical worldview, which is secular in its approach and its questions. Phenomena must have empirical, logical, and rational explanations. These two segments of the population have undoubtedly grown over time. Over the last six or seven years of survey data, the share of Americans who embraced the atheist or agnostic label hovered around 12 percent of the population, evenly split between each group.

There is another group that is a bit more amorphous and difficult to pin down: those who say their religion is "nothing in particular." What's notable is how large this group is compared with atheists and agnostics. In many years of the Cooperative Election Study (CES), at least 60 percent of all nones identified as nothing in particular. They amounted to 14 percent of the population in 2008, and in the most recent survey collected in late 2023, they climbed to 24 percent. The only response option that was more popular in the last sample was Protestant, at 30 percent. There are more nothing in particulars in the United States than Roman Catholics. It's hard to know for certain if there are any defining characteristics of this group. While scholars tend to classify atheists and agnostics as secular people, those who are nothing in particular could be described as nonreligious. They clearly don't have strong ties to religion, but there's not much evidence that they have embraced a principled secular outlook either.

The number of nonreligious Americans is significantly higher in the Cooperative Election Study compared with the General Social Survey. In the 2022 GSS, about 27 percent of respondents reported having no religious affiliation. In the 2023 CES, the share of nones was 35 percent. There's a fairly straightforward reason why the CES number is so much higher: The study gives people three options to indicate that they have no religion instead of one, which is enough to nudge more of them into saying that they are not religious. The key takeaway is not the actual percentage, though, but the fact that both statistics are rising at a very similar rate. The 35 percent that was nonreligious in the most recent CES sample was up from 21 percent in 2008. In the GSS, the increase was from 16 to 27 percent. The unmistakable statistical reality is that there are a lot more nonreligious Americans today than there were just fifteen years ago.

Which factors are most likely to indicate that an individual will identify as nonreligious? The first one that comes to mind for many is age, as younger people tend to be less likely to align with a religious tradition compared with their parents and grandparents. This is also evident in the data (see fig. 5.3). Among people born around 1940, the share who claimed to be atheist, agnostic, or nothing in particular was about 17 percent. That share continued to rise with each successive birth cohort. Among those born around 1960, the nonreligious share rose to nearly 30 percent. For those born in the late 1970s, the percentage was about 40 percent. However, it's worth noting that the trend line flattened out significantly among those who were born in the 1990s and 2000s.

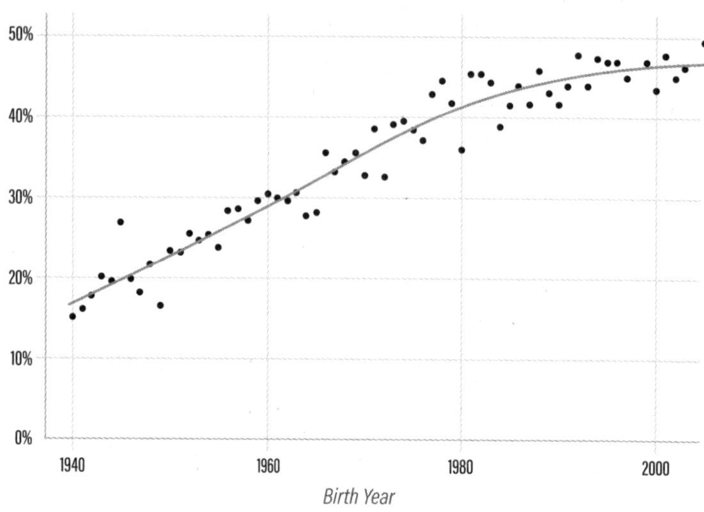

Figure 5.3 Share of the population that identifies as atheist, agnostic, or nothing in particular by year of birth, 2022–23

For instance, about 45 percent of people born in the mid-1990s were nonreligious, and the percentage rose only marginally for the youngest adult Americans. Looking at figure 5.3, if the percentage had continued to increase at the rate it did from 1940 to 1980, the share of nones would easily be north of 60 percent among today's college-age respondents.

The upshot of this is that age used to be an incredibly strong predictor of no religious affiliation, but the strength of its predictive power is clearly waning for younger adults. For instance, when comparing someone born in 1990 with someone born in 2005, we see that the likelihood that the younger person is nonreligious is only marginally greater than for the older individual. That is absolutely not the case when comparing someone born in 1965 with someone born in 1980. The data is pointing toward the conclusion that age is less predictive of nonreligious affiliation than it used to be.

Having said this, another factor in contemporary society may be even more powerful in pushing people to identify as atheist, agnostic, or nothing in particular: their political beliefs. Politics more so than age appears to be a strong predictor of nonreligious identity. That means Americans are becoming polarized along both religious and political lines.

(Non)Religion Is Downstream of Politics

In 2002, sociologists Michael Hout and Claude Fischer published an incredibly important paper titled "Why More Americans Have No Religious Preference: Politics and Generations." They note that the share of nonreligious Americans had doubled from the late 1980s to the late 1990s. Their conclusion as to the cause is straightforward: The rise of the nones is due almost completely to changes in the religious composition of those respondents who identified as politically moderate or liberal. Among conservatives, there was no appreciable change in overall religious makeup. Hout and Fischer contend that this movement can be explained by the rise of the Religious Right. More than two decades later, their final sentence seems prescient: "If the identification of religious affiliation with political conservatism strengthens, then liberals' alienation from organized religion may become, as it has in many other nations, fully institutionalized."[3]

What these two sociologists perceived in 2002 has only accelerated. In the following years, social scientists began to build a fuller understanding of the interplay between political partisanship and religious choice. Political scientist Michele Margolis argues that a key historical event was when the two parties began to move apart on issues related to morality and religious freedom, with Republicans embracing a more traditional view on issues like abortion and same-sex marriage and Democrats staking out more progressive stances on such issues.[4] Using several sets of survey experiments and extensive panel data, Margolis notes that individuals began to select into or out of religion based on their political preferences rather than their spiritual beliefs. She notes that it's no longer

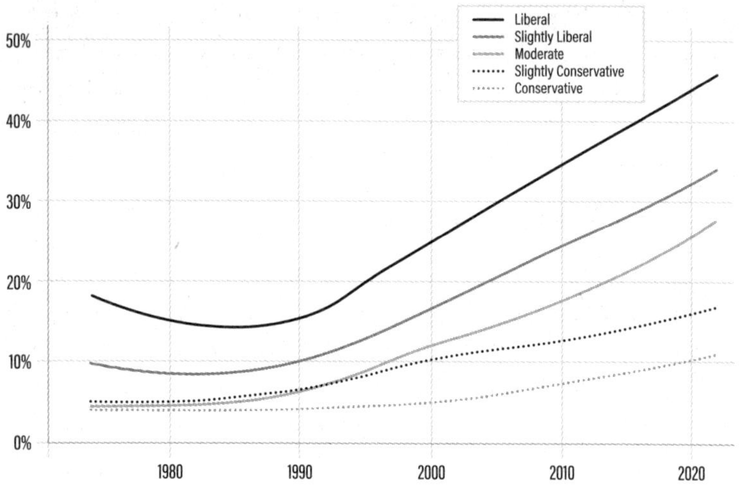

Figure 5.4 Share of the population that is nonreligious by political ideology, 1972–2022

accurate to think of political party affiliation as flowing out of other, bigger and more ultimate beliefs. Instead, it seems, political partisanship is the master identity of our lives, and everything else exists downstream of that. Thus, choosing what church to attend (or whether to attend church at all) is determined, in no small part, by how we orient ourselves in the political world around us.

In other words, politics impacts religion much more than religion impacts politics.

This reality comes through when doing just a bit of data analysis. If the sample from the General Social Survey is sorted by political ideology and religious affiliation, we see how big the gap has become among liberals and conservatives in the United States (see fig. 5.4). It's crucial to note that liberals were always more likely to report no religious affiliation compared with conservatives, but the gap was really only there for people who chose the most liberal option to describe their political ideology. In 1980, about 4 percent of conservatives claimed no religious affiliation compared with 6 percent who were moderate and 9 percent who identified as slightly liberal. But from the 1990s onward, the lines began to move far apart from each other, and the gap between those on the left and right sides of the political spectrum widened even further.

In the latest data, the share of conservatives who said that they were not religious rose to just above 10 percent for the first time, a five-point increase over the last forty-five years. For moderates, the share of nones rose much faster, reaching 28 percent in 2022. The gap between moderates and conservatives in 1990 was about 3 percentage points. In 2022, it was 18 points. However, the trajectory of liberals is unlike the trajectory of any other group. As early as 2005, the share of liberals who were nonreligious was 30 percent. It exceeded 40 percent by the mid-2010s. In the 2022 survey, about 46 percent of liberals were nonreligious. In the mid-1970s, the gap between the far left and far right sides of the American electorate on matters of faith (also known as the God gap) was 13 points. Today it is 34 points.

The political makeup of nonreligious Americans sheds light on a number of important points to consider when looking at long-term data trends (see fig. 5.5). The share of Americans who report no religious affiliation exploded over the last fifty years. It was just 5 percent in 1972, and today it's much closer to 30 percent. When a group is relatively small, as the nones were back in the 1970s, it's fairly easy for that group to be homogeneous in a number of dimensions—race, education, income, and politics. People self-selected into the group "nonreligious" because they knew what that group looked like and understood how their own personal demographics and opinions would square with the group. In other words, people had a pretty good idea of who the nones were in 1980, and many people didn't mind having that label describe them at the time.

It's highly unlikely that a social group that grows exponentially will maintain its basic political composition as it welcomes in tens of millions of new individuals. One almost expects by default that

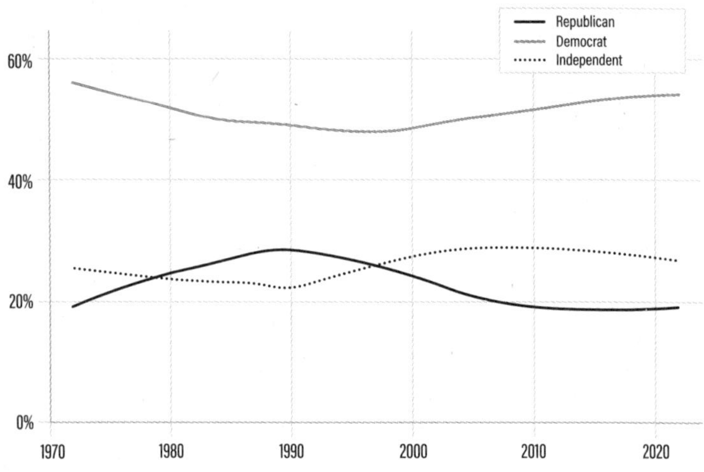

Figure 5.5 The political partisanship of nonreligious Americans, 1972–2022

such growth will upset the political equilibrium of any group. If one traces the political composition of the nonreligious since 1972, however, the story is one of tremendous stasis. In 1972, about 57 percent of nones said that they were Democrats, while about 20 percent were Republicans and the remaining 23 percent were politically independent. The share of Democrats never went below 49 percent in the following fifty years. It also never rose above 57 percent. The line is remarkably stable given the dramatic increase in the number of nones. Consider this: The share of Democrats in 1972 was 57 percent. It was 55 percent five decades later. The Republican share went from 25 to 19 percent, while the portion of independents shifted from 25 to 27 percent. In other words, the overall political breakdown of the nonreligious today is nearly the same as it was back in 1972, even as the group was more than five times larger in the most recent GSS survey.

How is this possible? It's not likely due to a strong communication network that can transmit messages among the tens of millions of nonreligious Americans. Christians have always had denominational networks and parachurch ministries to encourage adherents to stake out political and cultural positions. While there's no doubt that the Protestant landscape, especially the evangelical one, is more fragmented today than it has ever been, there is still a semblance of institutional structure. By contrast, most nonreligious people have no connection to or knowledge of groups like the Freedom from Religion Foundation and the American Atheists. Recall, also, that the biggest portion of nones are "nothing in particular," making up at least 60 percent of all nones in the United States. No group is working to organize this large and growing contingent of Americans who don't seem to care about religion one way or the other.

What then could be the reason why the overall political composition of the nones hasn't budged in the last fifty years? Returning to the work of Michele Margolis, we see that the average person increasingly understands that Christianity (especially white Christianity) is becoming more closely aligned with the Republican Party. Individuals who are left of center politically believe they are unlikely to find a house of worship that will align with their views. Thus, many find the most sensible option when it comes to religion is to leave it behind.

In essence, the public is sorting itself into camps based not on theological convictions but on partisan affiliation. Their religious identity is downstream of their partisan affiliation. The nones have continued to grow because Democrats and political liberals feel cast off by the increasing conservatism of American religion. While progressives might have found a welcoming house of worship among the Episcopalians or in the United Church of Christ two or three decades ago, those types of churches are disappearing rapidly in many parts of the country. And the congregations that remain are full of people who are closer to the end of their lives than to their preretirement years.

When looking at the polarization score of the nonreligious since 1972, it's clear that the nones were trending toward political

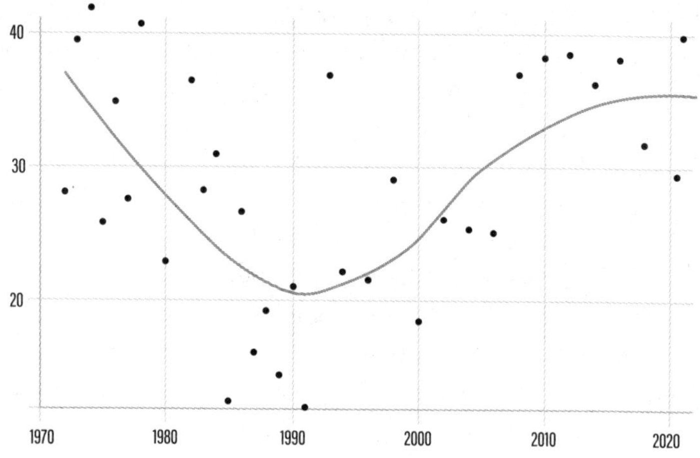

Figure 5.6 Polarization score of nonreligious Americans, 1972–2022

diversity between the 1970s and the early 1990s (see fig. 5.6). However, even when the nones were most politically diverse, nonreligious Democrats still outnumbered nonreligious Republicans by twenty percentage points. During the 1990s and through the 2000s, nonreligious Americans became increasingly aligned with the Democratic Party. By the time of Barack Obama's election in 2008, the polarization score of the nones had increased by a dozen points since its lowest point in 1990. In 1972, the polarization score of the nones was thirty-seven; today it's about thirty-five. But, again, recall that the nones were an incredibly small fraction of the country's population in the early 1970s, and today they are a larger group than evangelical Protestants or Catholics. A small, politically homogeneous social group is much less remarkable than one that maintains that unanimity *while* it rises to 30 percent of the population.

However, recall the three types of nonreligious respondents within the Pew Research Center framework: atheists, agnostics, and nothing in particulars. In terms of ideology, there is no group quite as homogeneous as atheists, though agnostics are not far from them in terms of both political partisanship and political ideology.

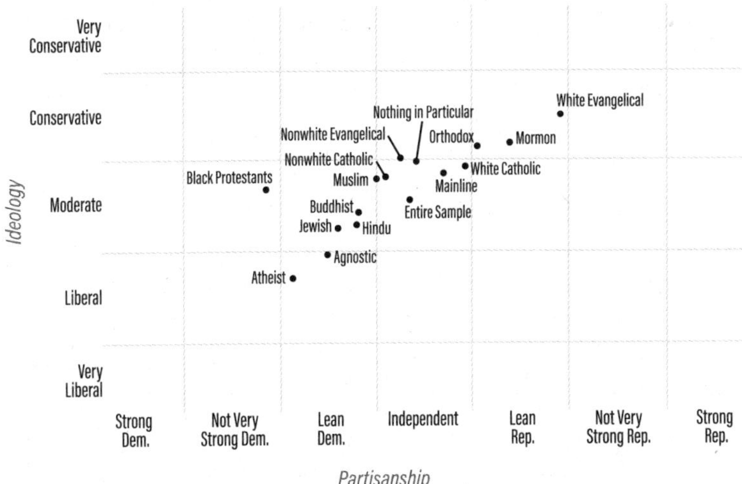

Figure 5.7 The political partisanship and political ideology of American religious groups, 2022–23

On a scale that runs from 1 (very liberal) to 5 (very conservative), the average score for atheists is 2.21 (see fig. 5.7). For agnostics, it's 2.45. By comparison, the overall sample average is 3.06. This indicates that the average American is just slightly toward the conservative end of the ideology spectrum. There is no group with a more liberal score on this metric than atheists. Agnostics are slightly more to the middle, but they are still significantly more liberal than the next closest group (Jewish Americans).

In terms of political partisanship, only one group is more likely to be to the left of atheists and agnostics: Black Protestants. The average Black Protestant scores a 2.34 on a scale that runs from 1 (strong Democrat) to 7 (strong Republican). Atheists have an average score of 2.62, and agnostics are 2.99 on this scale. By comparison, the average score across the sample is 3.86. This means that the average atheist is about 20 percent further to the left on political partisanship than the average American. There's no other way to say this: If white evangelicals represent the most conservative group, then atheists represent the most liberal group.

What may be even more striking is how different types of nonreligious Americans view the political landscape around them. The Cooperative Election Study asked respondents to place themselves on a seven-point ideology scale that ranged from 1 (very liberal) to 7 (very conservative), with 4 indicating a middle-of-the-road view. Then they asked respondents to place the Democratic and Republican Parties on the same scale. This battery of questions helps us understand how individuals see the entire political landscape. For instance, if someone scored themselves as a 4, Democrats as a 3, and Republicans as a 5, this individual sees the landscape as not at all polarized. But if someone put themselves at a 4 (meaning very moderate), Democrats at a 1, and Republicans at a 7, they perceive the political world as being as polarized as it can possibly be.

Since 2012, the average nothing in particular has been slightly to the left of center—just 0.17 points from being right in the middle of the spectrum (see fig. 5.8). They have deviated very little from that position over time. Their placement of both Democrats and Republicans is solidly left and right on the continuum but certainly not extreme. They put Democrats at 2.65, when 2.5 is halfway between very liberal and middle of the road. They put Republicans at 5.8, which is slightly more to the right than the midpoint of the conservative side of the spectrum but still reasonably in its center. This view of the political world is fairly moderate and does not see the political landscape as polarized.

Agnostics differ in two respects from the nothing in particulars. The first is that they see themselves much further to the left in terms of political ideology and growing more liberal with each passing year. On a scale from 1 to 7, agnostics put themselves at 3.20 in 2012, while nothing in particulars were at 3.83—a gap of about 0.6 points. In 2023, the average agnostic moved significantly to the left, to 2.79. The ideological gap between the average agnostic and the average nothing in particular was nearly a full point. The second difference is that agnostics used to see themselves as much more moderate than the Democratic Party. The gap in

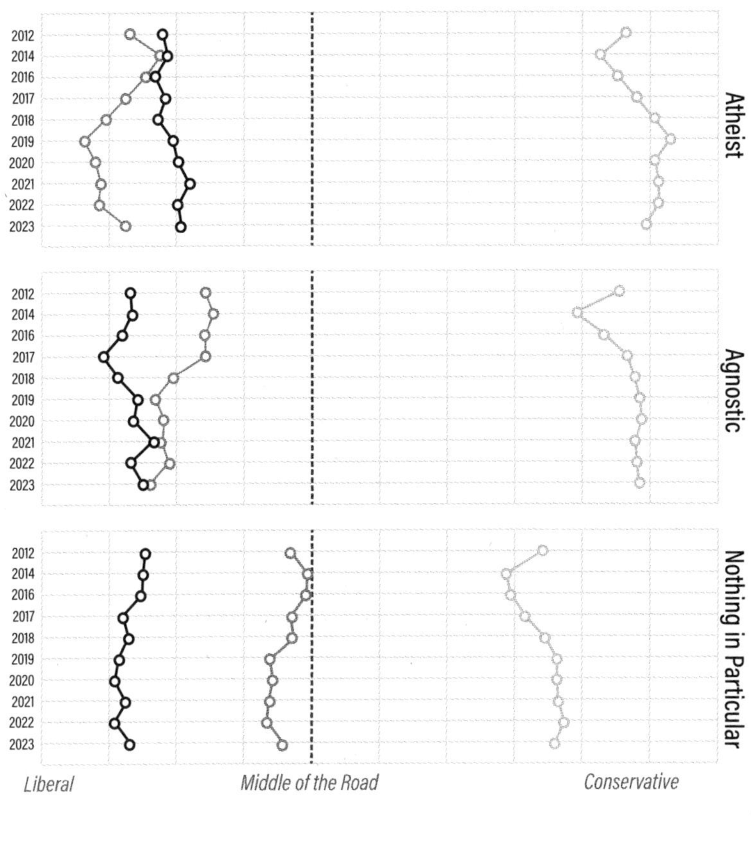

Figure 5.8 How atheists, agnostics, and the nothing in particulars see the political landscape, 2012–23

numeric terms was 0.56 in 2012. In the most recent data, that gap is 0.04—which means that the average agnostic sees no difference between themselves and Democrats. This is the result of agnostics seeing themselves as becoming more liberal over time, while the Democratic Party has moved toward the center.

Atheists have an entirely different perception of what is happening in American politics. Recall that the average atheist is more liberal than any other religious group. In 2012, on the scale from 1 (very liberal) to 7 (very conservative), atheists' score was 2.63, a position that was more liberal than agnostics have ever been. In 2019, the score was 2.30, the most liberal score of any religious group (including Muslims, Jews, and Black Protestants) in any year of the survey. In addition, atheists put the Democratic Party much closer to the center of the spectrum compared with both agnostics and nothing in particulars. That is, atheists believe that Democrats are much more moderate and becoming increasingly *less* liberal as time passes. Only one religious group clearly puts itself to the left of Democrats, and that's atheists. They also place the Republican Party further to the right than the other nonreligious groups do.

In other words, atheists view themselves as far to the left, while they believe that Democrats are becoming a middle-of-the-road party. Meanwhile, they view the GOP as about as conservative as can be. That view is akin to an activist group that seeks to pull Democrats toward its own preferred position while continuing to marginalize the views of Republicans as extreme. If white

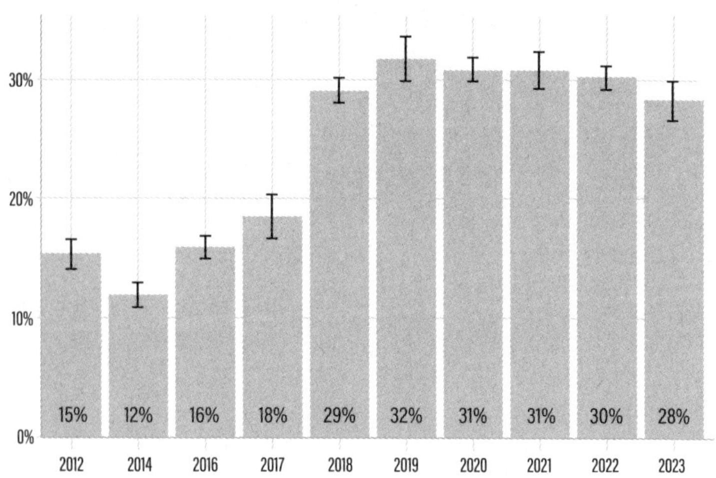

Figure 5.9 Share of atheists who see themselves as very liberal and the Republican Party as very conservative, 2012–23

evangelicals are the loudest political voices on the right, the same is true of atheists on the other end of the political spectrum.

To make this plain, I calculated the share of atheists who both described themselves as very liberal on the seven-point scale and described the Republican Party as very conservative (see fig. 5.9). Put simply, this is the share who see the largest ideological distance between themselves and the opposing party. When Donald Trump won the 2016 presidential election, only a small fraction of atheists had this incredibly polarized view—just about 15 percent. But after Trump took the oath of office in early 2017, atheists' views began to shift. By 2018, the share of atheists who had a polarized view had risen to nearly 30 percent. That's a doubling in just two years.

The good news, if there is any in this case, is that the percentage of atheists who say that they are very liberal and that the Republican Party is very conservative has stayed around 30 percent over the last five years. So there is no empirical data to conclude that atheists will further polarize in the years to come. There is simply no way to look at the data and not conclude that the number of atheists and agnostics has grown over the last fifteen years and that their politics has also changed significantly. They see a larger gulf between themselves and the opposing party than at any point in the recent past.

The Political World of American Atheism

Atheists are also the most politically active religious group in the United States. The 2020 Cooperative Election Study asked respondents if they had recently engaged in political activities such as attending a local political meeting, donating money to a candidate or campaign, and putting up a political yard sign. A score of zero indicates that someone was completely inactive with regard to politics, while a score of six means someone engaged in each action (see fig. 5.10).

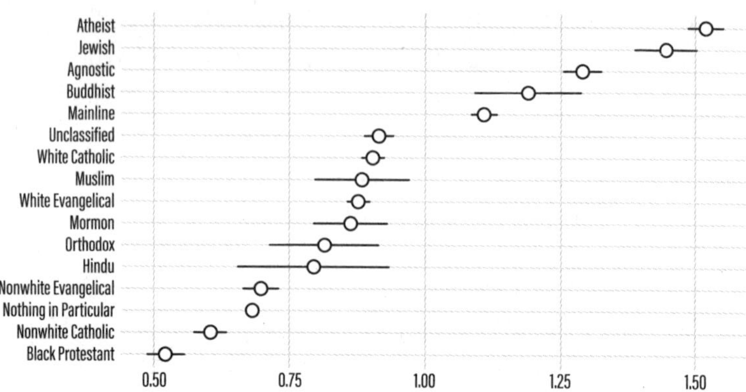

Figure 5.10 Average number of political acts (maximum of six) performed by religious group, 2020

The average number of political acts was 0.92, meaning that a typical American may have engaged in one political action during a presidential election year. A number of religious groups were close to this range, including white Catholics, Muslims, and white evangelicals. The most politically active group during the 2020 election cycle was atheists, who engaged in 1.5 acts on average. The only other religious group that came close was Jews, at 1.44 acts. Agnostics were the third most active, with an average of 1.29 acts. The share of atheists who donated to a candidate or campaign was 50 percent, higher than any other religious group and double the rate of white evangelicals. Yes, white evangelicals far outnumber atheists in the United States, but in terms of political activism, atheists punch above their weight. They want their voices to be heard, and they want a hand in directing the future of the American political process. If they can maintain this level of political activity while adding more members to their ranks in each election cycle, atheists may have more sway on party politics than any other group.

Atheists and agnostics have been particularly outspoken on issues of sexual orientation and gender identity. This is due, at least in part, to the fact that a significant share of atheists and

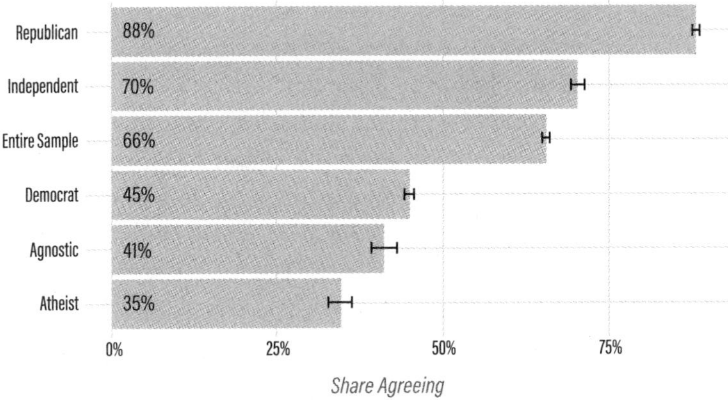

Figure 5.11 Share of respondents who agree that health care professionals should be banned from providing gender transition care to minors, 2023

agnostics do not identify as straight. In the 2023 Cooperative Election Study, about 87 percent of the total sample identified as heterosexual. Among atheists and agnostics, only 76 percent did so. In the same sample, 1.1 percent of respondents indicated that their gender was not male or female. Among atheists and agnostics, 2.5 percent so indicated. The discourse over gender transition has been especially prominent during the last several years, with the last skirmish in the battle focusing on whether minors should be able to receive gender-affirming care without parental approval. The Cooperative Election Survey from 2023 asked respondents whether they agreed that it should be illegal for any health care professional to provide a minor with medical care for a gender transition (see fig. 5.11).

Among the entire sample, two-thirds agreed that minors should not be able to go through a gender transition. Among Republicans, the number was 88 percent, but political independents weren't far behind at 70 percent. This is a topic that nearly evenly divides Democrats—45 percent of them agreed that minors should not be able to go through a gender transition. There were only two religious groups in which a majority believed that minors should be able to change their gender: agnostics (59 percent) and atheists (65 percent). By comparison, just 16 percent of white evangelicals supported gender transition for minors.

The view that gender transition should be permitted is part of a larger discourse inside politically active atheist and agnostic communities. This conversation came to a head in 2024 when famed atheist Richard Dawkins made several statements that seemed to indicate that he held a binary view of gender. He wrote, "Sex is binary as a matter of biological fact. 'Gender' is a different matter and I leave that to others to define."[5] When Dawkins began to make statements that hinted at his view of this issue as far back as 2021, he faced backlash from his own community. In fact, the American Humanist Association withdrew an award that it had bestowed on him in 1996 as "the humanist of the year," charging that he had "use[d] the guise of scientific discourse to demean marginalized groups, an approach antithetical to humanist values."[6]

Every social group has to establish and maintain boundaries to maintain its identity. Thought leaders in the community monitor the speech and actions of members and signal what behaviors and beliefs are acceptable or unacceptable to the community. If someone, especially an individual with a large following, transgresses those boundaries, they must be corrected or ostracized. Of course, this happens in Christian communities as well. For example, prominent former pastor Rob Bell wrote a book that questioned the traditional understanding of hell, and John Piper, a seasoned thought leader in evangelicalism, tweeted simply, "Farewell Rob Bell."[7] The same type of behavior occurs in the atheist community. While they don't all agree on a sacred text like the Bible, atheists still hold to an orthodoxy on a number of matters in political discourse. If one thinks that purification is something that happens only in religious groups, the case of Dawkins should serve as a stark example showing that orthodoxy is enforced and boundaries maintained in nonreligious spaces as well.

The Big Church Sort Is Nearly Complete

This chapter and the previous ones all illustrate the same point: There is a growing gulf in American religion. Among Christians (especially white Christians), the pull is unmistakably to the right. White evangelicalism has never been more politically unified than it is right now, and the Catholic Church is clearly headed in a much more conservative direction, as priests are almost uniformly conservative in matters of theology and ideology. While the mainline stands in the middle of the political spectrum, it continues its march toward irrelevance as its numbers and cultural power dwindle. Meanwhile, the nones have grown by leaps and bounds while maintaining an ideological and political purity that is uncommon for an amorphous group of atheists, agnostics, and nothing in particulars lumped together. Their politics are liberal (especially among atheists and agnostics), and they want to engage the political process as much as they can to reshape the Democratic Party in their own image, even if that's out of step with the views of more moderate Democrats who come from traditions like Islam and the Black church.

For decades of American religious history, churches have been places that harbored a diversity of political opinions. The data on this is clear: In the late 1980s, white American religion was incredibly evenly balanced. If one walked into a church during that time period, one would have found Democrats and Republicans sitting side by side in the pews. Evangelicalism had many holdovers from the New Deal coalition, while many younger members had begun to embrace the Religious Right. The Catholic Church had a strong faction of JFK Democrats, even as a growing faction of social conservatives strongly advocated for an end to abortion. The mainline, with its consistent political diversity, had lost some of its prominence in the prior decades but was still home to nearly 20 percent of the adult population. In other words, the American church looked much like the country as a whole.

Today, the Big Church Sort is nearly complete. The two Christian groups that have managed to maintain a robust membership, Catholicism and evangelicalism, have done so by drifting to the right. That's certainly made them a haven for cultural conservatives, but it has also tended to scare away people whose politics are further to the left. The mainline's commitment to ideological diversity has left its denominations on the verge of collapse. Meanwhile, the nones have gone from little more than a rounding error to representing the most significant cultural shift in the United States over the last three decades, becoming the default landing spot for political liberals who can't find a place in American Christianity.

Instead of the American religious landscape looking like a normal distribution, with lots of folks clustered around the midpoint, it looks like two mountains, one on the far left and one on the far right, with a chasm in between. Entire cottage industries on both the left and the right have cropped up to post video clips and memes mocking the other side. Prominent atheists produce content each day that could most appropriately be labeled "Crazy things that Christian leaders said today." Meanwhile, there's a whole ecosystem of "discernment bloggers" whose sole mission is to lampoon liberal mainline Protestant pastors and the secular left for things that they post on platforms like TikTok and X. Showing the extremes of the other side is a great way to generate likes, retweets, and maybe a few newsletter subscribers, but it's certainly no way to tamp down the heated rhetoric in American political discourse.

It's my contention that the American church can (and should) be one of the primary drivers of depolarization in the United States. However, due to a series of nearly invisible trends, religion in the United States is now more ideologically and sociologically homogeneous than it's ever been.

Up to this point, I've focused my argument on the political homogeneity within American religion. To kick off part 2, it would be prudent to dig into another fact about the average house of worship—it's more economically and sociologically homogeneous today than at any point in the last fifty years. The average American church is less and less the great meeting spot where blue-collar and white-collar people gather for common cause, and the average American Christian looks more and more like a person who did everything "right" in life—good education, middle-class salary, married with children. This simple fact is making the church both more politically unified and less welcoming to people on the fringes of society.

The Big Church Sort is not just evidenced on Election Day. It's also seen every Sunday when one looks at the types of people who choose to attend church and the types who choose to stay home. That's where we'll turn our attention next.

PART 2

SOCIAL AND POLITICAL POLARIZATION

6

The Great Reversal

THE BIG TAKEAWAYS

- Not only has there been political sorting in American religion, but there have also been additional divisions based on other demographic factors like education level, income, and marital status.
- Those at the bottom of the socioeconomic ladder are feeling left out and left behind by American religion—exacerbating political polarization and income inequality.

I was twenty-four when I took over the pulpit at First Baptist Church of Mount Vernon, Illinois. I had just earned a bachelor's degree and was halfway to securing a master of arts in political science. I was unmarried, living alone in a small apartment outside Carbondale, and had a few thousand dollars to my name. The vast majority of my parishioners on a Sunday morning had grandchildren who were about my age. Most people in the pews were at the age where they were collecting Social Security. While I would not describe the average member as wealthy, they were, by and large, financially comfortable.

In other words, I was a less than ideal fit for First Baptist. It was an odd experience to preach to a room full of seventysomethings on Sunday and then on Monday teach a class of college students who in many cases were under the legal drinking age. But our congregation made it work. I learned very quickly not to use any pop culture references in my sermons, unless they were about movie stars and musicians from no later than the 1970s. After having pastored the church for a year or two, I realized that very few men in their midtwenties spent so much time with elderly folks. It became a point of pride for our little band of worshipers, but I am sure that for anyone who walked in off the street it seemed strange to see the juxtaposition between the people in the pews and the person standing behind the pulpit.

The more that I dig into the social science data, the more I discover one of the true strengths of religion: It brings people into close contact who would never interact in any other setting. A thriving house of worship often has children sitting one row ahead of people who have celebrated their ninetieth birthdays. There are factory workers taking Communion right after doctors and lawyers. And as the previous chapters have shown, there was a time when plopping down in a pew on a Sunday morning could just as likely have put you next to a Republican as a Democrat. The church was seen as the great crossroads of American society—every age group, every occupation, and every political persuasion all uniting for a common cause on a regular basis.

In his classic work *Bowling Alone*, Robert Putnam writes in great detail about the tremendous benefit of being part of an organization like that. He calls the concept "bonding social capital."[1] Simply stated, bonding social capital is when you build strong relationships with others. You invite them to your home, you attend their children's birthday parties, they don't hesitate to ask you for a favor, and you don't think twice about asking them for help when you need it. When my wife gave birth to both of our boys, we returned home from the hospital to find a dish of soup on our doorstep, courtesy of some of the wonderful ladies at my church. That's a very tangible example of bonding social capital. People in my church coordinated doctors' appointments for older members and drove them to the hospital when they needed a blood test or an X-ray. Putnam argues that this type of social capital is essential for just "getting by" in American society.

But one of the benefits of American religion—the mixing of people from different parts of the socioeconomic spectrum and different walks of life—is disappearing. While the previous chapters focused largely on the political polarization that is sorting people into religious and nonreligious camps, another winnowing process may be just as insidious and overlooked.

Churches in the United States have become places where people who have done everything "right" are gathering. The pews are filled more than they ever have been with people who are college educated, middle class, and married with two children, while those who chose to take alternative courses are feeling less and less inclined to show up. Most religions emphasize that followers need to help those who are less fortunate, but unfortunately those kinds of people are becoming less inclined every year to come in close contact with regular attendees of religious services. The result is that religious people may see less opportunity to reach out to those who are living on the fringes.

In other words, religious practice has become a thing of privilege.

Are Wealthy, Educated People Less Religious?

If you've spent any time on the internet discussing religion, you've likely run into an atheist who thinks that anyone who believes in God is intellectually defective. They often tell people that they don't believe in "Sky Daddy" and don't need "fairy tales" to get through life. They may have read a bit of Karl Marx, or at least a few select quotes from *The Communist Manifesto*, and believe that

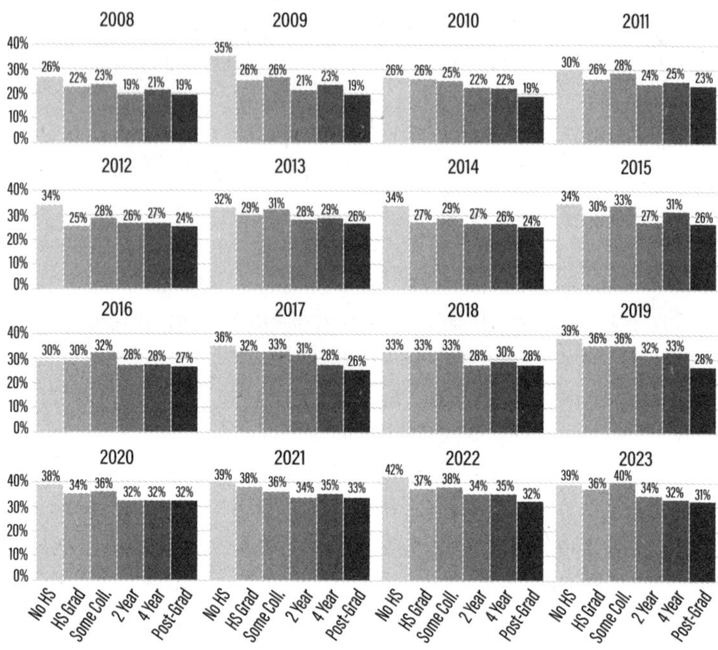

Figure 6.1 Share of the population that identifies as atheist, agnostic, or nothing in particular by level of education, 2008–23

religion is nothing more than a tool of oppression. Their favorite Marx quote is the oft-repeated maxim "Religion is the sigh of the oppressed creature, the heart of a heartless world, and the soul of soulless conditions. It is the opium of the people."[2]

Since the Enlightenment, it's been assumed that as people gain more rational knowledge over time, they will have less need for "superstitious" beliefs and will thus abandon religious belief and practice. That's the great claim of secularization, one that online atheists convey when they suggest that people with even a little bit of education should be able to see through religion's thin veneer and know it for what it actually is—a way to keep people happy in their subjugation.

However, in the United States today, the people who are the most likely to be religious are precisely the educated—those with undergraduate or graduate degrees. Those with high school diplomas or less are the least likely to claim any religious affiliation (see fig. 6.1).

The Cooperative Election Study has been fielded every year since 2008. Its real benefit is its sample size. When all its surveys are pooled together, nearly 632,000 individuals are included. This means the average poll includes nearly forty thousand respondents. I calculated the share of people who identified as atheist, agnostic, or nothing in particular over the last sixteen survey waves, but I broke it down into six levels of education ranging from not completing high school to having a graduate degree. The data is overwhelmingly clear: The people with the least amount of education are the most likely to identify with no religious tradition, while those with graduate degrees are the least likely to identify as nones.

This was true in the 2008 and 2023 datasets. In many years, the difference in the rate of nonreligion from the bottom end of the educational spectrum to the top is substantial. For instance, in 2014 and 2015, the share of those without high school diplomas who said that they were nonreligious was eight percentage points higher than those with a graduate degree (34 versus 26 percent). There are several years in the data where the difference in the share of people who identify as nonreligious (the nones) is ten percentage points from the least educated to the most. Now, it's also clearly the case that the nones rose among every education group over the course of the last sixteen years, but the education gap has not closed in any noticeable way. In fact, since 2017, the gap has never been less than five percentage points.

In other words, the rise of the nones isn't especially concentrated among those with just high school diplomas or those with graduate degrees. College-educated people are *more* likely to be aligned with religious traditions than those who stopped their formal education at twelfth grade.

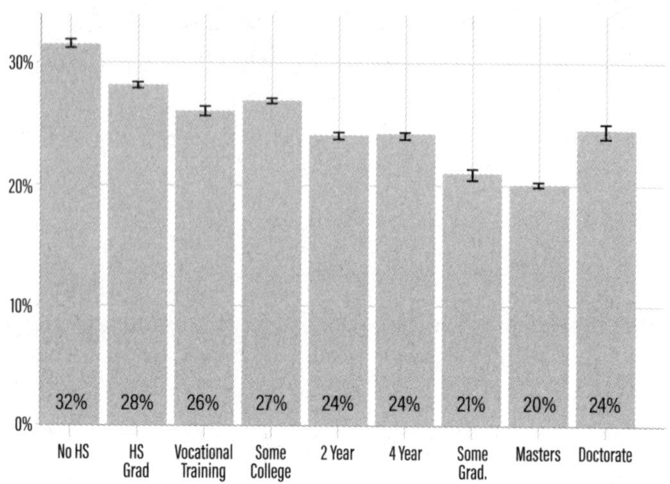

Figure 6.2 Share of the population that identifies as atheist, agnostic, or nothing in particular by level of education, 2019–21

Another dataset called the Nationscape Survey, which helpfully offers up levels of education that are unavailable in the Cooperative Election Study, replicates these findings. Nationscape was a weekly survey that was conducted from the middle of 2019 through the first week of 2021. An average sample was about six thousand respondents, so when all the surveys are added together, 477,000 participants are involved. While it's nearly impossible to look specifically at people with doctoral degrees in a typical sample because they make up a small fraction of the population, there are over 9,400 of them in the Nationscape Survey.

The same general trend found in the Cooperative Election Study reappears in this data (see fig. 6.2). For instance, about one-third of people without high school diplomas identified as atheist, agnostic, or nothing in particular. For every step of increase in education, the likelihood of identifying as nonreligious decreases. In this sample, just 24 percent of people who completed four-year college degrees were religiously unaffiliated. That's four percentage points lower than those who stopped at high school. From there, the percentages keep dropping. For people in the sample who earned master's degrees, just one in five of them were atheist, agnostic, or nothing in particular. This was the lowest percentage of any educational level. The nones rose a bit among those with doctorates, to 24 percent, but that's still the same level found among people with bachelor's degrees, and it's still significantly lower than among those with high school diplomas or less. Education is positively related to religion.

However, religious belonging is only one aspect of religiosity as a whole. It may be the case that more educated people say they are religious but don't actually attend religious services regularly. But that's an easily testable assertion using the same basic setup as the previous graphs. In every survey wave from 2008 through 2023, I calculated the share of people who attended religious services every week. Again, the conclusion is very similar to that of the prior analysis: Religiosity and education are positively correlated with regard to religious behavior (see fig. 6.3).

In 2008, the proportion of people with high school diplomas who were regular attenders of religious services was about 30 percent of the sample. Among people who had earned postgraduate degrees, 36 percent reported weekly attendance. The trend lines are positive in all sixteen years of data provided by the Cooperative Election Study: Those with higher levels of education are more likely to attend houses of worship on a regular basis compared with those who did not go as far with their studies. The differences here are statistically large too. In almost every year of survey data, those at the higher end of the educational spectrum are ten percentage points more likely to be weekly attenders compared with those who didn't complete high school. Educated people are much more religiously engaged—it's hard to look at the data and arrive at any other conclusion.

However, it's not so simple to determine *what* exactly about education makes one more prone to align with a religious tradition and attend church. A multitude of factors could create this

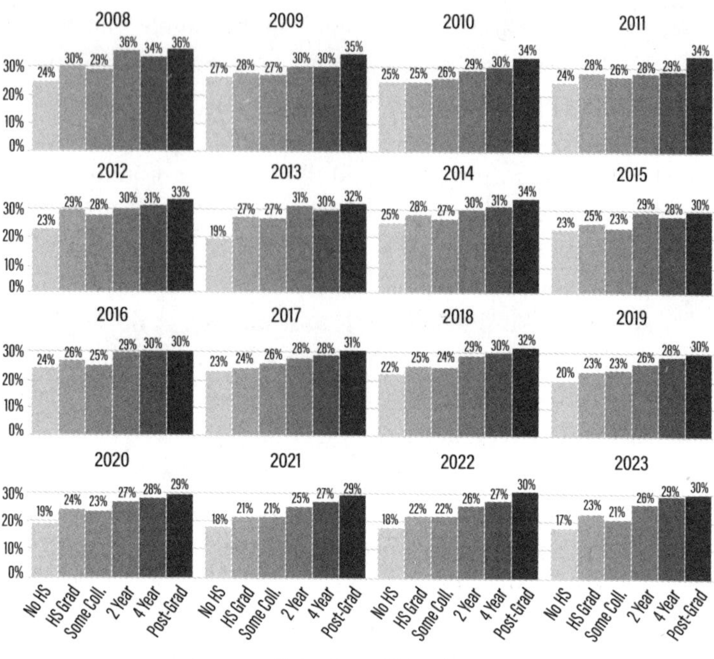

Figure 6.3 Share of the population that attends religious services at least once a week by level of education, 2008–23

outcome. One likely reason is fairly straightforward: trust. There is an incredibly strong relationship in survey data between higher education levels and belief that others can be trusted. There is also a strong connection between gaining more education and expressing trust in institutions like the media, big business, and, yes, religion. Yet it would be simplistic to say that increased education leads to a great level of trust that then results in people being more likely to attend houses of worship on a regular basis. It may be that people who grew up in high-trust environments are more likely to both go away to college and attend church on a regular basis. In other words, education may serve as a proxy for values inculcated to young people in their impressionable years that generate a posture in adulthood that leads to all kinds of positive outcomes, including increased education and church attendance.

Regardless of the causal chain, the result is the same. People with college degrees are more likely to say they belong to a religious tradition. They are also more likely to self-report regular church attendance. Many of them are likely able to identify the tangible benefits of being part of a religious organization. It's easier to find an insurance agent, a lawyer, or a doctor when one is highly connected to people in the community. It seems trite, but the best way for an individual to build ties to other people in the area is by joining one of the larger churches in town. But the corollary to this is that people at the bottom end of the educational spectrum are being left out of this network of helpful people who could be there for them when they bring a new baby home from the hospital or need help getting their children to school.

Education isn't the only significant factor when it comes to religious attendance. The data related to household income reveals a fascinating trend among the people who are the least likely to attend religious services.

The General Social Survey has asked about the household income of respondents since it first went into the field more than fifty years ago. To simplify this analysis, I separated the sample into those who reported that their income was in the top quarter of all earners in that year and those who were in the bottom quartile. I then tracked over the next forty-five years the share of each income group that reported never attending religious services in the prior year (see fig. 6.4).

In the 1970s, there was no appreciable difference in religious attendance between those at the bottom end of the income spectrum and those at the top end; about 10 percent of people were never-attenders, regardless of income. By the mid-1980s, the share of people at the top end of the income spectrum who were never-attenders was largely unchanged, at about one in ten. However, the same was not true for those in the bottom 25 percent, with almost

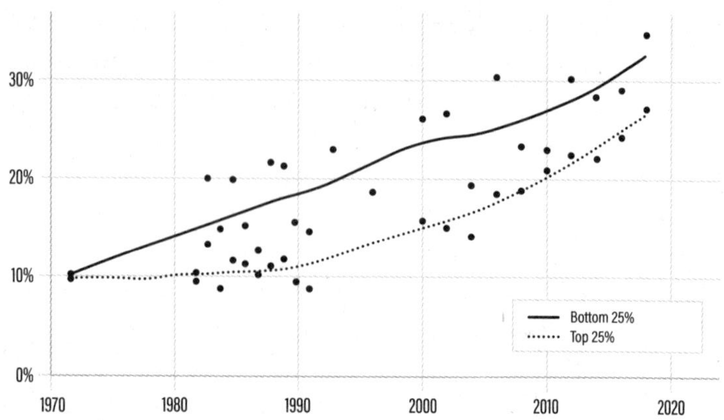

Figure 6.4 Share of the population that never attends religious services by income quartile, 1972–2018

17 percent saying they never attended services. The gap continued to persist over the next several decades. People with higher incomes were more likely to be in church compared with those with the lowest incomes. Both lines are rising, of course, as religion continues to recede, but the rise is more acute for people who are in the bottom quarter of income earners. In 2018, 35 percent of people in the bottom income bracket were never-attenders. That was about eight points higher than the top quartile. The poor are abandoning the church at higher rates than the rich.

But could the relationship between income and regular church attendance be a bit more complicated than that? For instance, is it the case that as income continues to climb, so does frequency of religious attendance? Or is there a point at which income is negatively related to religious behavior? To test that I combined several years of the Cooperative Election Study to create a sample size that was more than 170,000 people. The large sample size gives us a lot of granularity when it comes to income brackets, which is useful when trying to answer questions like this. The relationship between income and church attendance is more nuanced than many people assume (see fig. 6.5).

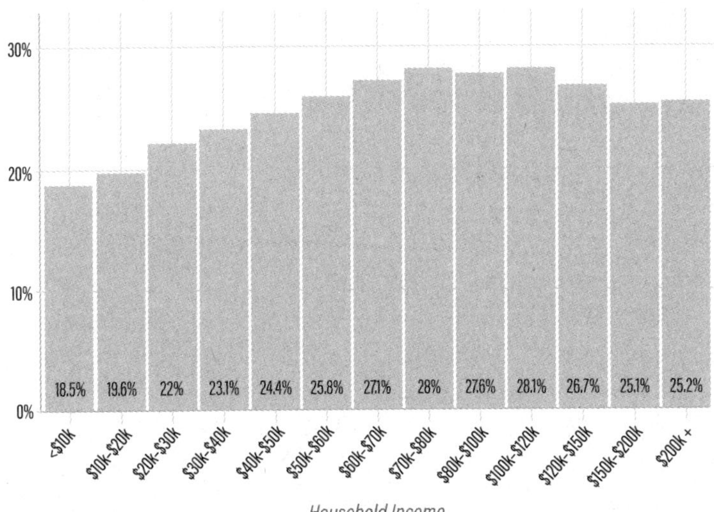

Figure 6.5 Share of the population that attends religious services weekly by household income, 2020–23

The people who are the least likely to attend religious services regularly are clearly those at the very bottom end of the income spectrum. For people who reported a household income of less than $20,000 per year, the share who attended on a weekly basis was less than 20 percent. However, as income increases, so does religious attendance. It climbs incredibly steadily across income brackets. An increase of ten thousand dollars a year in income correlates to a rise in church attendance of 1 to 1.5 percent. That trend is incredibly consistent from those at the bottom of the income spectrum to those making just over $100,000 a year. In this data, a person who makes $120,000 per year is ten percentage points more likely to be a weekly church attender compared with one who makes less than $10,000.

But the relationship between income and religious attendance is what statisticians call curvilinear—that means it looks like a rainbow. The percentages are lower on the ends of the spectrum and highest near the middle.

When household incomes rise past $120,000 per year, there's a clear drop in religious attendance. Just moving from one income bracket to the next highest leads to a decline in church attendance by 1.4 percentage points, and then attendance further decreases to just above 25 percent for people who report an income of at least $150,000 per year. Someone who makes $200,000 per year attends religious services with about the same frequency as someone with an income around $55,000 per year.

Thus, the relationship between income and religious attendance is not entirely straightforward. According to the United States Census Bureau, the median household income in 2022 was $74,580,[3] which also coincides with the highest level of religious attendance. In other words, the person who is most likely to be in church this coming weekend is someone who is right in the middle of the income distribution. They aren't overly rich, nor are they impoverished.

When the metrics related to income and education are combined into a single graph, the relationship between the two factors comes into much sharper focus (see fig. 6.6).

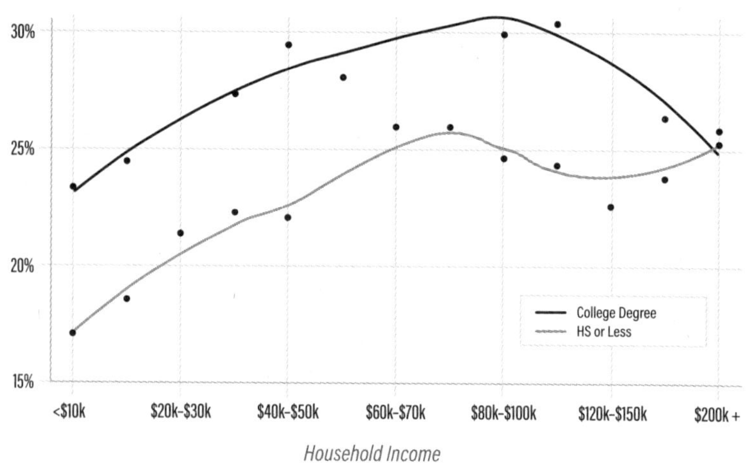

Figure 6.6 Share of the population that attends religious services weekly by education and income level, 2020–23

When comparing people who have high school diplomas with those who have college degrees, the only income level where religious attendance is similar is $200,000 per year. For reference, less than 1 percent of those surveyed put themselves in this income bracket. But across the rest of the income spectrum, there's a significant difference in religious attendance. For those who make right around the median income, about 30 percent of those with college degrees regularly attend religious services, while 25 percent of people with high school diplomas or less regularly attend. That five-point gap is fairly consistent throughout this data. Attendance does rise as income increases, but those with college degrees are more religiously active than those without degrees. That's an unmistakable conclusion here.

The Power of Connecting Across Differences

Returning to the discussion of social capital, it's important to mention that Putnam describes two types. There's the aforementioned bonding social capital. This capital results from building strong ties inside an organization or social group. It involves a sense of deep trust between individuals and helps people feel part of a community. Such capital is obviously important when it comes to religious organizations. A common phrase that pastors use is "We want to do life together." What makes that possible is bonding social capital.

The other type is even more germane to a discussion of the growing educational and economic homogeneity inside churches: bridging social capital. Instead of being about building strong bonds inside a social or religious group, bridging social capital is about making connections with people who are outside one's social group. It's about inviting new people into the fold—which is, of course, the key driver of many religious movements—but it also serves an incredibly important purpose for a functioning society. Putnam describes bonding social capital as being ideal for "getting by" and bridging social capital as all about "getting ahead." Bonding happens among people who are similar—social networks built on shared values and trust. But churches can also offer bridging social capital if they are diverse in background, profession, or socioeconomic status. If you need a dentist, a real estate agent, or a veterinarian, chances are good that someone in the pews might be able to help—but only if your congregation includes people outside your immediate circle. That may be an invisible benefit of religious belonging—it's been happening for thousands of years but is rarely discussed.

One of the most important aspects of American society is that the average citizen can have a real chance of moving up the economic ladder. There's a constant refrain among parents: "I just want my kids to have more opportunities than I had." The American Dream is simply that: coming from very little and building a happy, prosperous life. But which factors increase one's chances of moving up the socioeconomic ladder? One factor that is constantly referenced by economists is economic diversity, meaning people in a social space not sharing the same socioeconomic profile. Economic diversity has become increasingly rare in American life due to how stratified we have become over the last fifty years.

Where Americans live is directly related to financial capacity. Nearly every town, city, suburb, or village has its "good part" and its less desirable areas. People who tend to have higher levels of education and good incomes cluster in the same neighborhoods. There are downstream effects of that, of course. In most parts of the country, school districts are based on geography. That means that the children of more well-off parents do not go to the same schools as the kids who are raised in less ideal conditions. Even in the workplace, it's not common to find a blue-collar worker rubbing shoulders on a regular basis with someone who wears a suit and tie to the office every day. Lawyers tend to hang out with lawyers, and factory workers share a cafeteria with one another every workday.

At the turn of the twentieth century, the wealthiest man on earth was John D. Rockefeller. He had made his fortune in the oil business and at the time of his death had amassed a net worth of $1.4 billion—which was equivalent to 1.5 percent of the US gross domestic product. As Rockefeller's wealth grew, so did the public's fascination and scrutiny. Because of this, he became somewhat of a recluse. He would, of course, head to the office each day to keep an eye on his growing empire, but he would rarely venture out for a social occasion.

Despite all the hassle of leaving the house, Rockefeller was a faithful member of the Euclid Avenue Baptist Church in Cleveland, Ohio. In his sprawling biography of Rockefeller, Ron Chernow writes, "Aside from the spiritual pleasure of prayer, he was loath to give up contact with ordinary people, many of them old friends. The church retained many blue-collar members, enabling Rockefeller to chat amiably with a blacksmith or mechanic. Such everyday experiences increasingly eluded him as he withdrew behind the high gates of his estates."[4]

Rockefeller understood that attending church was a chance not just to engage in reverential worship but also to have close contact with the average person in his community.

The billionaire's intuition about the horizontal dimension of religion was confirmed by an important study published in the leading academic journal in the United States—*Nature*. A research team led by famed Harvard economist Raj Chetty examined data from over seventy million Facebook users. They merged this data with information from the income tax records of nearly forty million families to arrive at an incredibly detailed understanding of the economic conditions of the United States and how social connections are deeply intertwined with them.[5]

Chetty and his team developed a measure they called "friendship bias." It is a way to assess the likelihood not only of whether someone will come in contact with an individual from a different social class but also of whether they will form an actual connection across the economic divide. Their logic was that friending another individual on Facebook is a good indicator of more than just a casual acquaintance. The research team concluded that merely being in the same social space as another individual is not enough to generate any type of bridging social capital. Billions of dollars have been spent to create mixed-income neighborhoods or economically diverse student bodies at major universities, but no policy has been clearly successful in building the ties that are necessary to generate real economic mobility.

When they analyzed more than twenty-one billion Facebook connections among the forty million people in their sample, Chetty's team made a surprising discovery. The most likely places to generate durable and impactful connections were not neighborhoods, schools, or workplaces. Instead, a religious setting was the social space where the "friending bias" was most likely to occur. When people go to church, they tend to be a bit more open to making connections with the people around them compared with other spheres of life. A manager is more likely to accept a friend request from one of his subordinates if they have a relationship built through sitting in the same row during Sunday service.

What this research concludes is that poor children are significantly more likely to rub shoulders with their upper-class peers at Vacation Bible School than at their local school. In other words, houses of worship may be one of the last remaining engines of economic mobility. But considering the data indicates that churches, synagogues, and mosques are increasingly being attended by people with a college education and a middle-class income, we might wonder whether the societal benefit of religion is beginning to fade over time.

Marriage and Family Focused

As we've just seen, the types of people who are the most likely to regularly attend church are those who have earned bachelor's

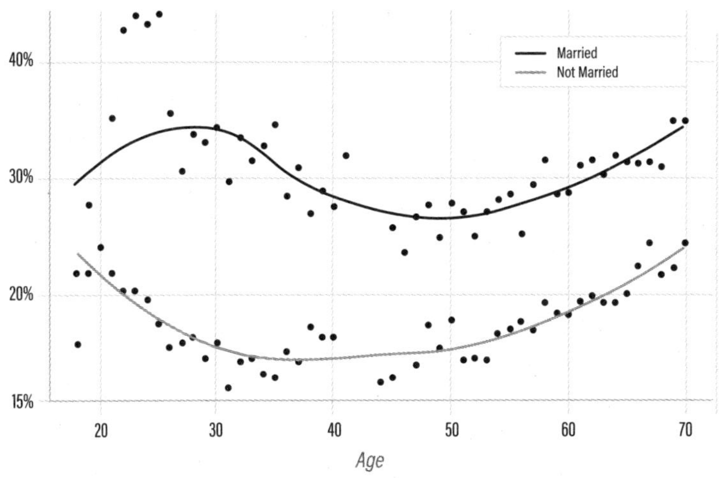

Figure 6.7 Share of the population that attends religious services weekly by age and marital status, 2020–23

degrees and have solid, middle-class incomes. That's the clear story that emerges from the data. But there's another part of the picture we haven't discussed yet when it comes to demographics and religious attendance.

There's a strong indication that marriage and family also factor into being active in a religious community. Every prominent religion in America places a strong emphasis on finding a suitable spouse, settling down, and having children. The Bible's command to "be fruitful and multiply" is often exhorted from the pulpit, and many houses of worship go out of their way to have vibrant family ministries. It's common for Sunday worship to have time set aside for "children's church," and many churches hold an annual youth Sunday when teenagers lead most aspects of the service. Thus, there's pressure, both explicitly and implicitly, for young people to follow the traditional course of marriage and family.

When survey data is analyzed related to marriage and religious attendance, it's incredibly clear that those who marry are more likely to frequently attend a house of worship (see fig. 6.7). No matter the age of the respondent, there is a huge chasm when it comes to religious behavior based on marital status. The gap is the smallest among the college-aged population—about 30 percent of married teenagers attend church weekly compared with 23 percent of those who aren't married. It makes sense that there's not a huge divergence in this part of the population, because marriage is a life event that typically doesn't occur for many until their midtwenties. But when we trace the trend lines through individuals who are in their mid- to late twenties, it becomes clear how powerful marriage is when it comes to church attendance.

Among thirty-year-olds in the United States today, nearly 35 percent of those who are married attend a house of worship on a weekly basis. Among thirty-year-olds who aren't married, church attendance is about half as frequent (around 16 percent). That difference is huge. Now, it is important to point out that the attendance gap between married and unmarried people begins to narrow for older people in the sample. Among those who are forty years old, church attendance drops to about 28 percent for those who are married compared with 15 percent for those who are unmarried. For people in their fifties, sixties, and seventies, the gap remains persistent and fairly large. In most cases, a married person is about ten percentage points more likely to be a weekly attender than an unmarried person of the same age.

Having children is another component in this equation. Family formation is taught as a central reason for people to marry, so married people without children may feel as though they have somehow violated the social norms of the community and become less likely to attend.

To test this theory, I separated the sample into four groups: those who are married with children, those who are married without children, those who are not married but have children, and those who are neither married nor parents. Tracing the share who report weekly religious attendance across the age spectrum is illuminating.

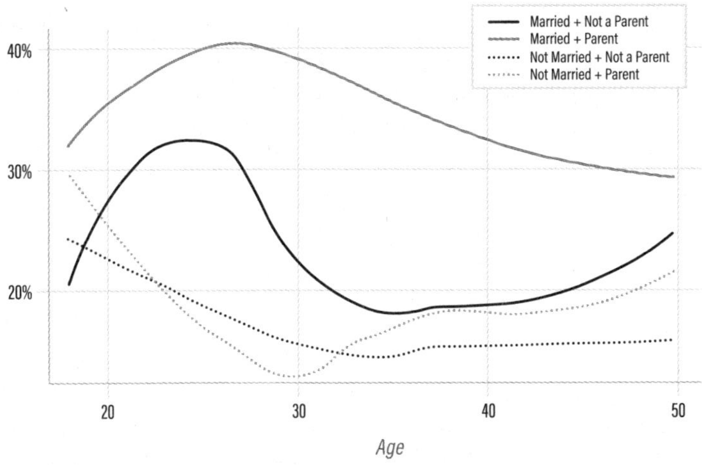

Figure 6.8 Share of the population that attends religious services weekly by age, marital status, and parental status, 2020–23

Figure 6.8 reveals a clear outlier (the solid line across the top): people who are both married and have children. The unmistakable conclusion is that people who are part of a traditional family structure are much more likely to attend a house of worship than those with any other combination of marriage and family. Among folks who are in their late twenties and are married with children, the share who attend religious services is about 40 percent. For comparison, among all American adults, about 25 percent report attending a house of worship regularly. The likelihood of married people with children attending religious services is consistently higher at every age in this analysis from twenty years old to fifty years old. Notice, however, that the trend line does begin to move downward at thirty years of age. A big reason for this is that the survey question asks whether a respondent is currently the parent or guardian of a child under the age of eighteen. What is likely happening here among those in their forties or older is that more and more of them have children who have become adults, and therefore they are no longer in the "married with children" category.

The group that is next most likely to be regular church attenders is people who are married and don't have children. However, the trend line for this group is worth some reflection. Comparing those who are in their late teen years with those who are twenty-five years old reveals a huge uptick in religious attendance, rising from about 20 percent to about 33 percent. But then notice what happens: the line begins to drop fairly quickly. Among people who are married but don't have kids and are in their midthirties, attendance bottoms out at just 18 percent. A possible explanation is that getting married in their midtwenties puts young people on the "correct" track by their community's standards. When married couples do not begin producing children by their late twenties, they are out of step with the prevailing wisdom among churchgoing people. As they continue to age and don't have children, their religious attendance continues to decline. This is powerfully suggestive that deviating from a community's standards can negatively affect maintaining an active role in that community.

For people in the sample who chose to not get married, attendance is lower, which logically follows from figure 6.7. The only age range in which marital status is less consequential is from late teens to early twenties. It's readily apparent from this data that people who aren't married by thirty years of age are much less likely to be regular attenders. However, it's crucial to point out that there is a statistically significant difference when it comes to parental status. Among thirty-year-olds who are unmarried and have no children, about 15 percent are weekly religious attenders. For those who are single parents, church attendance is even lower—just 13 percent. When looking at the entire range of ages in the data, that is the group of people who report the lowest level of religious attendance. According to this data, the person who is least likely to regularly attend a house of worship is a single parent in their late twenties or early thirties. The person who is the most likely to be a weekly attender is from the same age group but is married and has children. The difference in weekly attendance rates is about twenty-five percentage points.

The Problem of Socioeconomic Polarization

A significant amount of literature in the field of economics points toward a constellation of factors that lead to better life outcomes. Having a stable home life with a supportive spouse and a devotion to children leads to higher income with fewer hours worked. Also, the connection is incredibly robust between earning a college degree and finding more satisfaction in life—even after controlling for other factors. Regular religious attendance is, of course, part of this equation too.

It's hard to distinguish the causal factors, however. For instance, does regular religious attendance drive up the likelihood of pursuing higher education and starting a family? Or do having a higher level of education and being part of a traditional family increase one's likelihood of regular religious attendance? It's likely they are mutually reinforcing. People tend to surround themselves with individuals who have gone through life following a pattern similar to theirs. Thus, a white-collar worker may hear colleagues talking about church activities and want to be part of that community as well. Or growing up in a house of worship where one is surrounded by people who are well educated and tend to have strong families may lead one to subconsciously pursue the same path. Regardless of the causal direction, the result is the same: American churches have increasingly become places where people who have done everything "right" gather on a regular basis.

There are tremendous implications of this in terms of the future vitality of American society. As previously described, religious organizations are ideal spaces for people who are at the lower end of the economic spectrum to find a pathway into the middle class. However, that can be true only if those folks who are struggling financially actually make it to church on a Sunday morning. When

I was in college, I attended a local Methodist church that was organized by several members of the religion faculty at the college. They used St. Paul's to give upper-division ministry students a chance to preach to a live audience. The church was liturgical in its worship, following a pretty standard order of service that included responsive reading, recitation of the Apostles' Creed and the Lord's Prayer, hymn singing, and a short homily. It attracted an interesting mix of college students, faculty, and folks from the community.

One Sunday morning, I got to church five minutes before the service began and sat in a row of chairs near the back. As the pianist was playing an intro song, I saw a young man come in through the back door who looked like he was in his early twenties. Following closely behind was a girl who looked to be about his age, and she had a baby on her hip. They slid into the very last row of the sanctuary. One of my favorite parts of worship at St. Paul's was called "the prayers of the people." The worship leader would read a written prayer that asked God to bless our country and its leaders and for peace throughout the world. After that, attendees could voice a prayer so that the rest of the people gathered could hear. We typically heard things like "We are traveling this week; please pray for our safety" or "My sister has been diagnosed with cancer; pray for her to recover." After each prayer, the worship leader would say, "Lord, in your mercy." And the congregation would respond with "Hear our prayer."

That is such a powerful way to pray because at that moment you feel every single person around you pulling for you and your prayer request. Typically, this section would last only a minute or two. The congregation might repeat "Hear our prayer" four or five times. This is what was happening in the worship service I was attending—the typical exhortations to pray for someone who was sick or struggling. But right before the worship leader was about to move into the next section of the service, I heard the voice of that young man who had walked in late with his girlfriend and their baby. He said simply, "Could you all please pray for me? I lost my job, and I don't know if I can afford our rent this month." The worship leader said, "Lord, in your mercy," and we all said forcefully, "Hear our prayer." Then the service proceeded as it typically would. There was a short sermon, we took Communion, and the service ended with a blessing from the pastor.

As people were gathering up their things and getting ready to head out, one of the older gentlemen in the congregation made a beeline to the back of the sanctuary. He walked up to the young man standing behind me who was struggling to pay the rent and said to him, "Son, if you need a job, you can come work at my lumberyard tomorrow." The young man responded enthusiastically, and they agreed to meet the next morning to work out the arrangement. The Lord works in mysterious ways, right? If someone speaks a tangible need into a community of folks who have been taught to be helpful to those around them, miraculous things can happen.

But what the data suggests is that fewer and fewer young families are attending religious services with each passing year. Instead, church has become a place for people who don't need that type of help. They have earned college degrees, they have middle-class incomes, and they have a spouse and some children. Let me be clear on this point: I don't believe American religion has intentionally told single mothers that they don't belong in their communities. I don't think that any pastor has made it clear that only those with bachelor's degrees are allowed to sit in the pews on Sunday. I've seen no evidence that churches are telling folks that dropping a hundred-dollar bill into the collection plate is a necessary requirement for membership. But even so, religious spaces are becoming less diverse.

While the majority of this volume has focused on ideological polarization, socioeconomic polarization is just as real and may be more caustic than the fact that churches have sorted themselves into Republicans and Democrats. In local communities, religious organizations have often been places where a person could find a friend or two to help them overcome their loneliness. They were places where addiction recovery groups could meet to offer support. They were places where people who had fallen on hard times could find a little bit of support to get through them. Religious organizations spent decades building a kind of invisible social safety net to make life just a little bit easier. But it seems as though more and more of the people who could tangibly benefit from being part of a faith community are increasingly likely to be disengaged from religion.

The Big Sort that's going on in American religion is running on two tracks that seem to reinforce each other. Many churches have emptied out in the United States because a certain subset of people headed for the exits, and it wasn't just a random sample of the country that never returned. The people who left fall into broader categories—politically moderate or liberal but also unmarried, divorced, or without children. Many of those who don't go to church now are folks who went no further than a high school diploma and are often teetering on the brink of financial precarity. Who is left in the pews? It's largely Republicans in many houses of worship. And the data says that the most likely churchgoer is a college-educated, married parent who makes about $80,000 per year.

It seems that ideological sorting and sociological sorting have become mutually reinforcing trends in many congregations. The belief that government should provide fewer social service programs and institute lower tax rates is certainly a centerpiece of the Republican Party, and that viewpoint goes unchallenged when a person who holds it rarely interacts with people who are most in need of social service support. As mentioned previously, there's a tremendous difference between hearing about people struggling with financial insecurity on social media and sitting next to someone in a Sunday school class who confides that they are struggling to pay their children's medical bills. While John Rockefeller could have certainly learned about the day-to-day lives of blue-collar workers by reading the local newspaper, he understood the value of hearing directly from someone he had known for decades.

Mark Twain once remarked, "Travel is fatal to prejudice, bigotry, and narrow-mindedness."[6] But I think one doesn't have to journey hundreds of miles to get that same experience. In theory, all one has to do is attend a local church. Standing shoulder to shoulder with a bank president and a factory worker while reciting the Apostles' Creed can do wonders in creating understanding and compassion across the class and political divides facing the United States. However, the American church is continuing to fall far short of that ideal, becoming a haven for those whose lives have stayed on a narrow path. This had led to an increase in misunderstanding, a decline in empathy, and a further fraying in our social fabric.

7

How the 1990s Paved the Way

THE BIG TAKEAWAYS

- In the 1990s, American religion changed dramatically. The share of young people who identified as Christians declined, and nonreligion rapidly increased in popularity.
- A confluence of events, including the end of the Cold War, the rise of political polarization, and the widespread adoption of the internet, drove these changes.

When I talk to my students about the state of American religion and politics, I feel as though they get tired of hearing me say, "It hasn't always been this way." Most of them were born after the year 2000 and came of age in a world where evangelicals and Catholics were becoming more conservative with each passing year, the mainline tradition was largely irrelevant, and a growing number of their peers were declaring themselves to be atheists, agnostics, or attached to no religious tradition in particular. I have to spend a great deal of time (and generate a whole lot of graphs) to paint a picture of the American religious landscape that has only a passing resemblance to the current state of affairs.

Most of my students don't know that even into the late 1980s, white American Christianity was nearly evenly divided between Democrats and Republicans. The average Southern Baptist church had a strong contingent of Democrats and Republicans; that was also the case for the United Methodists and the local Catholic parish. At the same time, the share of Americans who identified as nonreligious didn't really change much between the early 1970s and 1990. It was just about one in twenty Americans. To be a none during the Reagan administration was to be in a very distinct minority.

But something happened in the early 1990s that set us on the course that led to the religious polarization we are experiencing today. The way my college students understand religion is a direct result of this period of incredible political and religious upheaval.

One of the things that college professors try to do in the classroom is tie things back to foundational concepts in our discipline. In this case, there is a simple concept called "path dependence." Simply put, path dependence posits that the reason things are the way they are today is because of how they were a year, a decade, or a century ago. We inherit the plausibility structures of institutional constraints set in place by previous generations. Remember the church that I began pastoring back in 2006 with the declining membership? Many of the problems I faced leading that congregation were due to decisions that were made by the church council long before I was even born. My students (and my own children) are going to be living with the fallout of all the shifts that happened in American society during a ten-year window of time that they can only read about in history books.

The only way for us to begin to dig out of the morass of our hopelessly divided political and religious climate is to understand

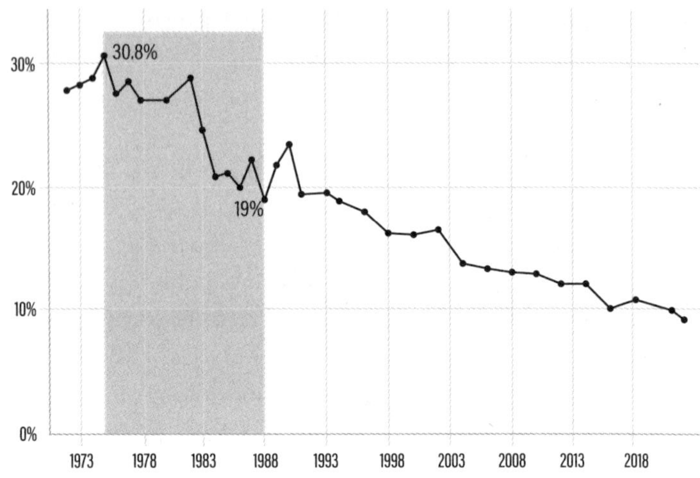

Figure 7.1 Share of the population that identifies with a mainline Protestant tradition, 1972–2022

how we got here in the first place. A variety of forces came together in the 1990s—including the end of polite politics and the advent of internet access in American homes—that worked in concert to begin driving us apart. The aim of this chapter is to begin sketching out a vision of why the nones began to rise, how Catholics and evangelicals began to veer to the right, and how all that led to the collapse of the moderate middle.

Evangelicals Rise While the Mainline Declines

The first indication that things were shifting in American religion happened as early as 1975, long before the nones began to rise and nearly two decades before evangelicalism would hit its apex. In the mid-1970s, the largest religious tradition in the US, without a doubt, was mainline Protestantism. Nearly 31 percent of all adults were aligned with a mainline denomination. By comparison, evangelicals made up just 21 percent of the population. In fact, evangelicals were the third largest religious group behind

Roman Catholics, who composed about a quarter of the population. The nones were 7 percent of the population.

But in the late 1970s and throughout the 1980s, the share of mainline Protestant Americans dropped at an incredibly rapid rate (see fig. 7.1). According to the General Social Survey (GSS), they were 31 percent of the population in 1975; just thirteen years later, they were only 19 percent. No other religious group in the fifty-year history of the GSS lost that much of its membership that rapidly. In terms of population numbers, the mainline had about sixty-six million adherents in 1975, and by 1988 that number had dropped to forty-three million. In thirteen years, the mainline lost about twenty-three million members. By comparison, the current membership of the Southern Baptist Convention and the United Methodist Church combined is about eighteen million. It's staggering to consider just how many people left the mainline in terms of the overall religious landscape.

In 1975, mainliners outnumbered evangelicals by nearly 10 percentage points (see figs. 7.1 and 7.2). In 1988, about 27 percent of the population was evangelical Protestants and only 19 percent was mainline. Evangelicalism had increased by six points, while the mainline had declined by nearly twelve points in this incredibly formative period.

Of course, there were other tremendous changes in the cultural and political landscape during this period. Scholars generally agree that the Religious Right had begun to coalesce around the Republican Party by the late 1970s. When Republican Ronald Reagan challenged the incumbent Jimmy Carter in the 1980 election, the fresh shoots of conservatism in white Christian politics began to blossom. During the Reagan era, the general public turned significantly rightward after the Democrats had enjoyed a firm grip on the levers of power for decades. As conservatism began to take hold among the white populace, it began to manifest in electoral victories, but it also began to reshape the American religious landscape.

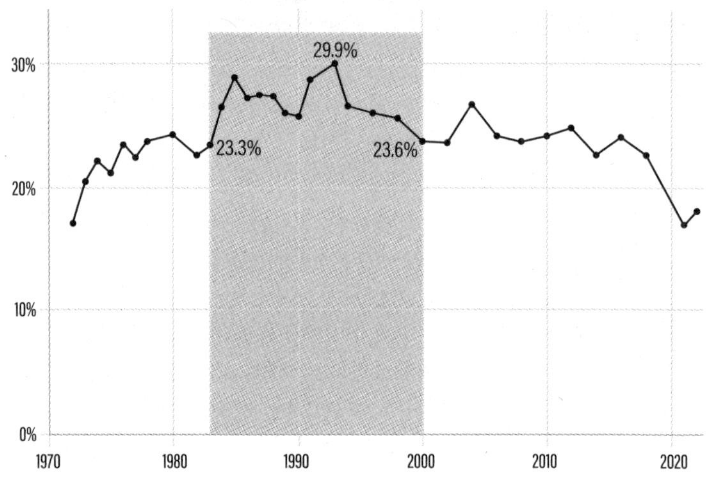

Figure 7.2 Share of the population that identifies with an evangelical Protestant tradition, 1972–2022

Evangelicalism began a rapid ascendance, and the mainline began to fade into the background.

The rapid decline of the mainline through the last years of the 1970s and throughout the 1980s led directly into another drastic shift in American religion: the rapid ascension of evangelical Christianity. Between 1973 and 1983, the shift in evangelicalism was small, the share of evangelicals increasing from 20 to 23 percent. By the time Reagan comfortably won reelection in 1984, the evangelical share of the population had risen to 28.7 percent. After seesawing up and down for the next few years, the percentage bumped up again in 1991 to 28.6 percent and then inched up even further in 1993 to 29.9 percent.

In the large sweep of American religious history over the last five decades, the data points to this conclusion: American evangelicalism was at its apex in terms of size in 1993. While it's impossible to know for certain why 1993 is a magical year, it's fair to assume that the wave that began building during the heyday of the Religious

Right and Republicans' ascendance in national politics took a while to work its way through the general public.

I was born in 1982 and grew up in a Southern Baptist church throughout the 1990s. I have had dozens of conversations with people around my age who grew up in similar church environments. A constant sentiment comes up: "Evangelicalism was an all-encompassing subculture in our youth." From a data perspective, that's an empirically defensible claim to make. Nearly a third of all Americans identified as evangelical by the mid-1990s—that's about seventy million evangelicals. This made it easy for adherents to build their own bookstores, clothing lines, and music festivals. For those of us who grew up in the evangelical subculture, it felt as though we could live in an evangelical cocoon and be protected from the outside world.

While Democrat Bill Clinton managed to win the White House in 1992, evangelicals still had a tremendous influence on politics throughout his two terms. His administration negotiated a series of compromises with conservatives on issues like welfare reform and the military's "don't ask, don't tell" policy. Clinton's signature statement on abortion was decidedly moderate: "safe, legal, and rare." These positions were emblematic not of a Democratic administration that was trying to pull the country hard toward the left but instead of a White House that understood how powerful evangelicalism was in the public square.

Yet despite its rapid ascendance, what may be even more stunning about the rise of evangelicalism is how quickly it fell back to earth. Between 1983 and 1993, evangelicals grew 6.6 percentage points. Between 1993 and 2000, they gave back nearly all those gains and returned to about 23–24 percent of the population, staying at this number between 2000 and 2014. In other words, in the broad trends of evangelicalism in the United States, the burst between 1983 and 1993 can be seen as little more than an anomaly. Evangelicals were in the midtwenties in terms of population share before this time and returned to nearly the same spot after this ten-year outlier.

A Generation in Religious Flux

The drop in the share of mainline Protestants between 1975 and 1988 and the subsequent rise of evangelicals between 1983 and 1993 are statistical backdrops for what may be the most substantial long-term development in American religiosity. The 1990s became an inflection point for American religion that may never happen again. Between 1991 and 1998, the religious composition of young adults underwent a tectonic shift. When the survey sample is isolated to just those between the ages of eighteen and thirty-five, a portrait emerges of a generation in religious flux.

Tracing the religious composition of young adults between 1972 and 1991, we see an unremarkable trend line (see fig. 7.3). In 1972, about 86 percent of this age cohort aligned with some type of Christian group. For the next twenty years, that number never went higher than 87.5 percent and never went lower than 82 percent. Things were about as steady as it gets when it comes to polling data about religion. The line for the nones was similarly

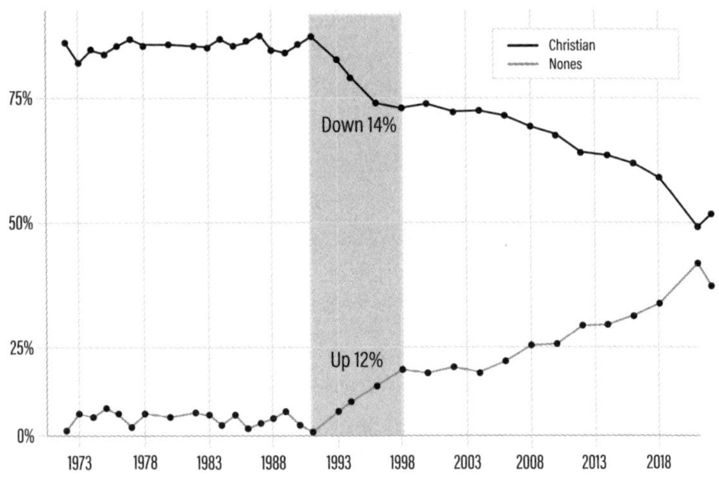

Figure 7.3 The religious affiliation of eighteen- to thirty-five-year-olds, 1972–2022

consistent. For almost every year during this stretch, the share of young people who reported no religious affiliation was 11 percent. Some years it dropped to 9 percent, and other years it was as high as 13 percent. But looking at the long-term trend, we see that the religious composition of young adults was substantively the same in 1991 as it was in 1972.

However, the share of young adults who said that they were Christians dropped incredibly quickly and consistently between 1991 and 1998. In 1991, 87 percent was Christians. Five years later, the number was down to 74 percent, and it continued to decrease through 1998, when it ended up at 73 percent. It stayed at that number for the next eight years or so before slowly beginning to decrease again. During this same time frame, the share of young people who said that they were nones shot up (see fig. 7.4). It was 8.1 percent in 1991, more than doubled to 17 percent by 1996, and then increased to 20.5 percent during the next two years.

Let me restate that. Between 1991 and 1998, the share of eighteen- to thirty-five-year-olds who said that they had no religious affiliation went from 8.1 to 20.5 percent, while the share who were Christians dropped from 87 to 73 percent.

It is my contention that nearly everything we've observed in American religious demography over the last twenty-five years flows from the changes that occurred during this crucial period of the 1990s. Over the past several decades, nothing has happened in the US that was as dramatic as this shift in the overall religiosity of young adults. To put this age group in context, the oldest members of this cohort were born in 1956, while the youngest members were born in 1980. That means that almost all of them are done with childbearing now, and most of the children born to this cohort are in their twenties and thirties. The people represented in figure 7.3 were raised in a culture that was overwhelmingly Christian. But many of them in turn did not raise their children in the same religious environment they were raised in. Their offspring were at least twice as likely as they were to be raised in nonreligious households.

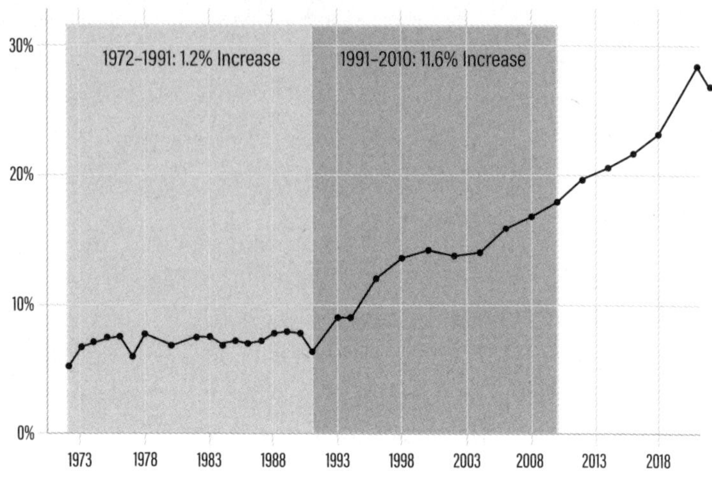

Figure 7.4 Share of the population with no religious affiliation, 1972–2022

The strongest predictor of your current religion is the religion in which you were raised. It doesn't take a huge leap in logic to realize that the long tail of this rapid shift was the increase in the nones that has been happening for the last thirty years.

Of course, indications of this significant youth shakeup began to appear in the full sample as early as 1991. Remember, the nones were an incredibly small portion of the American population throughout the entirety of the 1970s and 1980s. In numerical terms, they increased just 1.2 percent between 1972 and 1991. Yet in the next nineteen years, the share of Americans with no religious affiliation rose nearly 12 percentage points, from 6.3 to 17.9 percent. From 2010 to 2022, when the most recent data was collected, the nones rose another 10 points, landing at just below 27 percent.

It's easy to see how the 1990s served as a crucial inflection point in the trajectory of Christianity and nonreligion in the United States. The decade almost serves as a hinge—the country's faith landscape looked much different in the 1980s compared with the

2000s. The ruts that were formed by Americans (especially young adults) in the 1990s are almost impossible to escape now. Young people coming of age in 2025 will find it much easier to fall into the patterns that were established by their parents and grandparents than to carve out a different religious landscape for themselves and the next generation.

When Being Moderate Became a Liability

Once we begin to piece these trend lines together in chronological order, a much clearer picture of religious polarization begins to take shape. While the mainline had been hemorrhaging members at a steady rate since the 1950s, there is a real inflection point in the data in the late 1970s and early 1980s when the mainline began to lose members at an increasing rate. That's when the first fruits of the Religious Right began to take hold. While Ronald Reagan was not himself an evangelical, he made a concerted effort to court the conservative Christian vote when he ascended to national politics in 1979. At this same time, the most influential voices in American religion began to shift away from the United Council of Churches and toward a number of prominent televangelists who were decidedly evangelical in their theology and conservative in their politics.

For scholars of the Christian right, a consensus has begun to emerge that voices like Jerry Falwell and Pat Robertson had a cleaving effect on the American religious landscape. Many Americans felt like the old choices of evangelical or mainline Protestantism were no longer relevant. One had to be either a full-throated member of the Religious Right or not religious at all. The moderation of the mainline was seen, for the first time, as a real political liability, and trend lines in the data reflect this new reality. Yes, the share of Americans who identified as evangelical surged during this period and reached an all-time high in 1993, but demographics are a zero-sum exercise; for every percentage point increase in one group, another group has to lose market share. That was exactly the case for the mainline—their numbers dropped by nearly ten points in the next decade. But all those losses in the mainline weren't just shifting to evangelical membership rolls. This is also the time when the nones began to experience tremendous growth as well.

This is a point that is often missed when discussing the impact of the Religious Right on the American religious landscape. Yes, it absolutely led to a surge in the share of Americans who aligned with an evangelical tradition, but it also led to a rapid weakening of other major Protestant denominations, and it pushed a growing number of Americans, especially young adults, to no longer align with any religious tradition at all. That's the rub of any religious organization: The messaging that may appeal to a certain subset of the population may repel another part of it. When looking at the data, that's the only conclusion that makes any sense: The Religious Right divided American religion and society.

But what was unique about this period of time in American history that such a cleaving effect could take place? For one, the early 1990s saw a gigantic shift in the balance of power on the world stage. For nearly forty-five years, the United States was locked in the Cold War with communism. The Soviets were constantly maneuvering to penetrate America's defenses. In the early days of the conflict, searching for citizens who were sympathetic to the Marxist cause became a national pastime. One way political leaders tried to insulate the United States against the communist threat was to remind Americans of their religious virtue. While communism was a belief system that had no room for God, Congress made it clear that the United States was, at least at a cultural level, a religious country. The phrase "under God" was added to the Pledge of Allegiance by a joint resolution of Congress in 1954, right as the McCarthy hearings were winding down. About a year later, President Dwight Eisenhower signed a bill that required all coins and paper currency to include the phrase "In God We Trust."

To be an outspoken atheist during the height of the Cold War was to marginalize oneself from society.

That sentiment began to fade somewhat as the Cold War evolved from a boiling conflict into little more than a simmer. However, when the Berlin Wall came down in November 1989 and the Soviet Union formally dissolved in 1991, it may have led to a not-so-subtle shift in the way Americans (especially young adults) thought about their own religion. It would have been impossible for most people to be publicly nonreligious in the 1960s without fear of being blackballed in their workplace. By the mid-1990s, the thought of someone losing their job or their friends because of their lack of belief in God was more and more remote. Now, it was possible to be an atheist and not be a communist. The inherent link between the two had largely been severed, and the door to social acceptance of atheism began to open ever so slightly.

The fall of communism was not the only major event that may have changed the religious landscape. In domestic politics, rhetoric had taken a decidedly divisive tone. Even throughout the 1980s, elected members of Congress maintained cordial relationships with people across the aisle. The book *Tip and the Gipper*, by political commentator Chris Matthews, describes the cordial relationship between Democratic Speaker of the House Tip O'Neill and Ronald Reagan. However, by the early 1990s, the era of good feelings was over. Newt Gingrich, one of the rising members of the Republican coalition, believed that the only way for the GOP to regain the majority in Congress was by trampling on the unspoken rule that it was better to look the other way when a political opponent was engaging in ethically murky behavior. Gingrich knew that the only way to wrest power was by throwing bombs at every leader of the opposing party, even if doing so rankled members of his own.

The title of a 2018 article in *The Atlantic* tells the whole story: "The Man Who Broke Politics."[1] Gingrich made it his mission to topple the Speaker of the House using whatever means he saw fit.

When Tip O'Neill resigned his post, he was succeeded by another Democrat, Jim Wright. Gingrich caught wind of a report that Wright had signed a sweetheart book deal with a publisher in his home district that would give him a significantly larger royalty than was typical for authors. Additionally, the report indicated that many Wright supporters had made bulk orders of the book to direct additional income toward Wright without strictly violating ethics rules. Things like this had been occurring for decades in Congress among members of both parties, and it was generally accepted that unless the behavior was egregious, it was better to look the other way. However, Gingrich didn't accept the unspoken rule and knew that he had enough leverage to force Wright to vacate his position. In May 1989, Wright gave a speech to the House of Representatives announcing his resignation. He stated,

> It is grievously hurtful to our society when vilification becomes an accepted form of political debate. And negative campaigning becomes a full-time occupation. When members of each party become self-appointed vigilantes carrying out personal vendettas against members of the other party. In God's name, that's not what this institution is supposed to be all about.[2]

In the long arc of congressional history, this is the moment when things began to shift. Politics became about doing whatever it took to win, even if it meant ruining a colleague's reputation. Gingrich's approach was, without a doubt, successful. The proof was in the 1994 midterm elections, when the Republicans took control of the House of Representatives for the first time in nearly forty years. As a reward, the GOP quickly chose Gingrich to be their speaker. The Gingrich model of politics was handed down to other Republican members of Congress and was adopted by members of the Democratic Party as well. Of course, dirty politics were only reinforced by the rapid adoption of a twenty-four-hour news cycle that was constantly looking for content to fill the airwaves.

In 2001, political scientist Geoffrey Layman published *The Great Divide*, a book that portended the growing chasm between Democrats and Republicans on matters of faith. A few years later, Robert Putnam and Dave Campbell described this schism in greater detail and popularized a catchy phrase for it: the God gap.[3] It was not considered odd for a politically left-of-center young person to be a regularly attending Southern Baptist in 1980, but it was becoming much more difficult for that to be the case fifteen or twenty years later. The seeds of political division and polarization that were planted in the early 1990s began to bear fruit in the arena of American religion. Young people who were both religious and left of center politically felt that they had to make a choice between their ideology and their theology. As the 1990s wore on, more and more of them chose the former and sacrificed the latter.

It's necessary to weave the Religious Right into this larger narrative as well. Remember, evangelicalism hit its numerical peak in 1993, right as young people were heading for the exits of American religion. While the religious landscape of the 1970s and 1980s offered a panoply of options for Protestants, those began to shrink as the 1990s began. Evangelicalism was now the loudest voice in the room when it came to matters of theology. Leaders like Falwell and Robertson knew that the best way to activate their base was to nudge them toward the rightward edge of their theological comfort zone. While the Southern Baptists had taken a moderate position on abortion in 1971, allowing for abortion in a number of cases, including rape, incest, and saving the life of the mother, the Religious Right would not allow for such a pragmatic position. In 1993, the Southern Baptist Convention passed a resolution that permitted abortion only if the mother's life was in danger. Sociologist Ruth Braunstein notes that "backlash against a radical form of religious expression leads people to distance themselves from all religion, including more moderate religious groups that are viewed as guilty by association with radicals."[4] With dwindling cultural cachet for the mainline, the average American understood

Protestant Christianity to be clearly conservative and trending further to the right.

What is hanging over this entire discussion, however, may be the most important factor and the hardest to accurately measure: the proliferation of the internet.

According to World Bank data, in 1991 about 1 percent of American homes had internet access. By 1998, that had expanded to 30 percent. By 2001, at least half of all households could access the World Wide Web.[5] In just a decade, half of Americans had adopted a single technological innovation. The impact on American religion is hard to assess. For the first time, an individual could do a quick online search and find hundreds of thousands of resources to help them understand the faith in which they grew up but also the beliefs and practices of other traditions. It became easy not only to find flaws in one's own theology but also to point to inconsistencies in others' beliefs. While the internet led millions of Americans to explore ways to express their spirituality, it also may be true that millions may have found their way to a religious community through a quick online search.

The internet also allowed people to find others who shared their bents on all manner of things—comic books, movies, politics, and (of course) religion. There were, without question, atheists living in the Bible Belt in the 1950s. But given the political climate and the Red Scare, they likely kept their views to themselves at the dinner table and in the breakroom. But with the internet came scads of chat rooms and message boards where people could find like-minded individuals. The right website could make a person realize that they weren't the only atheist in East Tennessee. Finding other people who shared their views may have nudged them into mentioning their religious persuasion to close friends or family. The number of those who identified as atheist, a trend that was almost completely flat from the early 1970s through the early 1990s, shot upward in the years that followed.

When Americans Began to Leave Religion

Changes in the social world are the product not of just one or two phenomena but of several factors moving in concert. Yet the result is clear: Americans began to walk away from religion in very large numbers at this pivotal point. This is a statistical reality that many Christians need to grapple with when thinking about the role of fiery and divisive rhetoric. Yes, it may be effective in bringing in a certain subset of the American population—it did seem attractive to more conservative mainline Protestants in the 1980s and 1990s. But at what cost? It certainly weakened many of the most prominent and geographically disbursed denominations in the United States. It also drove hordes of young adults away from religious identity and belonging. The fact that the share of eighteen- to thirty-five-year-olds who described themselves as non-religious was twelve points higher in 1998 than in 1991 is evidence of that cleaving effect.

Remember the concept of path dependence? Where we are today is a direct result of events that occurred decades ago. Many young adults who took the General Social Survey in the early 1990s went on to have children in the decade that followed. The strongest predictor of one's current religious tradition is the religious tradition of the household in which one was raised. That means that millions more children were raised in non-Christian households in the 1990s and 2000s than one generation prior. That's one of the primary reasons the nones have continued to rise: Many millennials and members of Generation Z were not raised with any religion to begin with.

These young people by and large were raised in an American religious climate where the only concept they had of Christianity was that it was politically conservative. That is exactly the type of student I see in my classroom each semester. The hollowing out of American religion will continue unless young people are made aware of two central facts. The first is the one previously mentioned: It hasn't always been this way. Reminding my students that religious movements in the United States have advocated for both conservative and liberal causes can go a long way in helping them see the full diversity of American Christianity. The second fact is that path dependence is certainly not destiny. Just because the American religious landscape is incredibly polarized now doesn't mean it has to stay this way. Making my students aware that there are politically conservative atheists and politically liberal evangelicals gives them permission to swim against the current.

What is also a potentially hopeful sign for the next generation is that many of them seem to have been raised with a type of religious tabula rasa—a blank slate when it comes to any type of deep understanding of the landscape of Christianity in the United States. Remember, a growing number of them were raised in entirely nonreligious households. That means they weren't exposed to the divisive rhetoric that was pervasive in the 1980s and 1990s. They don't know about the televangelism scandal of Jim and Tammy Faye Bakker. They just don't understand religion that well at all. Which means they don't see the ruts of path dependence, and so they might feel empowered to create a new and hopefully less polarized version of American Christianity.

8

How Religion Became a Tribal Identity

THE BIG TAKEAWAYS

- The data indicates that a growing number of people are identifying as religious to denote a cultural or political identification, not because of a deep faith in God or the Bible.
- This has driven more people to leave religion, as they see it not as a community of believers navigating life together but as nothing more than a way to describe whom people vote for.

As we've just seen, the 1990s were an incredibly crucial time in American religion. Droves of young people left Christianity behind, and more of them began to embrace the label "nonreligious." The rise of the Religious Right and culture war rhetoric helped to recast religion, making it different from what it was in previous periods of American history. Now, an increasing number of Americans began to see religion as primarily political. It wasn't about one's theological beliefs about Jesus, the Bible, or the atonement. It wasn't about wrestling with big existential questions, such as why people suffer or how to forgive those who have wronged us. Instead, religious identification became more strongly linked to whom one voted for on Election Day. It became a type of shorthand for political views, not theological positions.

The simple question "Are you religious?" is not straightforward anymore. Dozens of times a year, completely unprompted, people try to answer that question for me. Many of them get tangled up in knots when they try to verbalize how they view themselves in relation to religion. I hear the following lines from lots of people:

"Oh, I'm not religious, but I am very spiritual."

"I like the idea of Jesus. I just think churches are corrupt and unnecessary."

"Christianity lost me when it became so wrapped up with politics."

"I just don't really feel the need for any of it."

I find those statements fascinating. I have devoted the last fifteen years to puzzling through how people think about religion and their own faith journeys. They often spend just half a second thinking about it before giving me a quick (and often dismissive) sentence about how they feel about religion and spirituality. But those quick asides offer scholars a peek into how average Americans understand the concept of religion and orient themselves toward it.

"Being religious" is an incredibly amorphous concept. It's hard to quantify religious beliefs, to pin down what counts as a spiritual act. People's religiosity can rise and fall during certain life stages, and whether someone defines themselves as religious or not on a survey could be largely affected by their emotional state in that moment.

That said, I believe the data shows that Americans are increasingly understanding religion in a very clear-cut way: as a tribal marker for politics. Thus, to call oneself a Christian (or even more specifically, an evangelical) is to make a statement about one's political worldview, not really about one's local church or spiritual walk. That may be the most dangerous outcome of the events that unfolded in the 1990s as described in the previous chapter: Religion became so deeply intertwined with politics that it is impossible to extricate it.

For many people who grew up in evangelical churches that took the idea of a personal relationship with Jesus Christ seriously, there was no moment more important than the altar call. After the preacher spent twenty to thirty minutes exhorting the congregation to accept Jesus into their heart, an organist would play a hymn like "I Surrender All" while the pastor waited for someone to leave their pew and join him at the altar to say the sinner's prayer. For me, that was an emotional experience. I was aware of my own sinfulness and my desire to get right with God, to be washed clean of my transgression. But I have to wonder whether some young people these days feel called to come forward but hesitate, thinking, *If I come forward on this Sunday, does that mean I have to be a Republican?* When religion is deeply connected with politics, it's impossible to know how much that connection impedes some people from pursuing a life of faith.

At the same time, there seems to be a rapidly spreading phenomenon of people who say they are religious and believe that religion is an important part of their lives even while they have essentially no connection to a local church. They are the opposite of the hesitant people described above; they want to say they are born-again because of the cultural connotations of that phrase more so than because of theological conviction. It's a way to tell friends, family, and pollsters that they are conservative on issues related to sexuality and gender. It means that they like the values espoused by Republican politicians and they agree with elected officials when they decry what they see as an attack on Christianity in the United States. It's religion as a tribal marker. It's being religious in name only.

To make this case empirically, it's helpful to start by explaining how social scientists think about measuring the concept of religion, because it may be one of the most difficult questions in social science. To be sure, certain activities are clearly religious. Attending a service at a house of worship, going through a bar mitzvah, or entering a marriage that is officiated by an imam are undoubtedly all religious actions. But there are a lot of gray areas too—activities that are highly religious for one person but much less so for someone else. For instance, if a high school student says "Please help me" to no one in particular before taking a test, is that a religious act? If an individual chooses not to eat for a day or two as a type of cleanse or in search of clarity, is that a spiritual activity?

A couple years ago I shared a graph on social media that analyzed responses to the question "How often do you feel thankful for your blessings?" Among people who attended religious services at least once a week, over 80 percent reported feeling thankful for their blessings at least once a day. Among those who never attended religious services, daily gratitude was much lower—less than 40 percent felt thankful on a daily basis. The responses offered a window into how a basic idea like thankfulness is seen by some as being inherently religious. A common thread in the discussion was that the concept of thankfulness assumes that there is someone or something that provides blessings and thus people can't be thankful if they don't believe that a provider exists. One person wrote that they were "thankful for my many privileges, not my blessings." Having grown up in the church, I had never even considered the fact that those things weren't blessings.

Part of my work is trying to figure out what people think when they are asked the question "Are you religious?" Does one person's mind immediately gravitate toward the certainty they feel that God exists? Does someone else automatically start counting in their head how many times they went to church in the last year? Does another person latch on to their family's attachment to the

Catholic Church because of their Italian or Irish lineage? All three are absolutely appropriate ways to think about religion, by the way. This is an area where social science tries to be value neutral. If someone says they are religious because they have a deep belief in a higher power yet they are not attached to any religious tradition and don't attend a house of worship, their religiosity is just as valid as that of a Muslim who has engaged in the five daily prayers for their entire life. Individuals determine their religion on their own terms.

That said, academics who study religion must apply a methodological framework to what it means to be religious with the goal of making it a bit easier to grasp, measure, and conceptualize. Using survey research to analyze religion in the United States is a relatively new scientific venture, with the first longitudinal instrument (the General Social Survey) first being fielded in 1972. Since then, we've made great strides in using quantitative methods to get a general sense of the contours of American religion. The utility of such an endeavor is pretty clear. If we never developed some fairly stable measures of religiosity, it wouldn't be possible to answer even basic questions such as whether the United States is more religious today than it was thirty years ago or whether younger people are less religious than older people. Of course, significant methodological disputes persist in the scientific community about the best ways to measure religion, but a general consensus has emerged that religion likely manifests in three ways: belief, behavior, and belonging.

Belief, Behavior, and Belonging

Religious belief is the understanding that one holds in one's mind about the existence of God, heaven, hell, angels, demons, and so on. But religious belief extends far beyond the simple question of whether God exists. How someone conceives of the divine is incredibly important too.

In their book *America's Four Gods*, Paul Froese and Christopher Bader argue that while most Americans believe in God, the way that they conceive of a higher power varies dramatically. The four categories they created are (1) the authoritative God, who is engaged and judgmental; (2) the benevolent God, who is engaged by loving; (3) the critical God, who keeps a tally of our sin but doesn't use it against us; and (4) the distant God, who is largely removed from human affairs.[1] How people see the divine can have a tremendous impact on how they act in familial relationships and ethically ambiguous situations. There's also been work that has shown that referring to God as male is strongly related to political conservatism, especially among women.[2] In other words, religious beliefs can have a foundational and often subconscious impact on how we see the world—such as whether we see good things in our lives as "blessings" or "privileges."

Behavior is the most tangible aspect of religiosity and thus is usually the easiest to measure. In almost every major religious tradition, regularly attending corporate worship is strongly encouraged. That's certainly the case with every flavor of Christianity, Judaism, and Islam. Muslims are also required to engage in five daily prayers (called *salat*) while facing Mecca. Of course, there are other types of religious behavior—for instance, prayer, giving tithes or offerings to charitable causes, and doing works of service in the community. These examples tend to be harder to measure than simple religious attendance. From a social science perspective, attendance may be the most consequential aspect of the religious experience because it is, by definition, a social enterprise. Gathering with people who share a set of beliefs has all kinds of ancillary benefits to the individual, the community, and the larger democracy.

Religious belonging is of incredible consequence to those who study religion through the lens of survey data. Only a handful of questions tap into this question, with the most popular being "What is your present religion, if any?" There is not a standard set of response options, but the approach that seems to be increasing in popularity is the one used by the Pew Research Center. It offers a dozen possible responses ranging from Protestant to Catholic to Latter-day Saint. The list also includes world religions like Islam, Buddhism, and Hinduism. Three options are nonreligious: atheist, agnostic, and nothing in particular. A final option is "something else," and respondents are provided space to enter words that describe their religious affiliation. How someone answers this question speaks volumes about how they understand their social identity and where they fit into the broader social, religious, and political context of the United States.

Take, for instance, an individual who was raised Catholic—who was baptized in the church and went through all the confirmation classes. However, as this person entered adulthood, they began to drift away from the church. They haven't been to Mass in several years, even skipping Christmas and Easter. When reading through the options, this person has to pause and deliberate over whether they are Catholic or something like "nothing in particular." If they check the box next to Catholic, they are saying something very important: "I still see myself as Catholic, and I feel a connection and kinship with fellow Catholics." They are declaring where they fit in American society. According to the religious behavior metric, they are not religious, but when it comes to where they belong, they are still a Christian.

This is why religious belonging has become a shorthand for someone's tribal identity. It helps researchers understand how respondents answer the age-old questions "Who are my people?" and "Who aren't my people?" In this case, the respondent is saying that they are not a none, and they find no common cause with that group, even though their religious attendance is the same as a none's.

From a purely social science perspective, these three dimensions of religiosity (belief, behavior, and belonging) are not equivalent. One is purely individualized—belief. I tend to think of this as the vertical orientation of religion. The other two are about how religion manifests in a social context and are clearly more horizontal. But that's not to say that belonging and behavior are the same measure. One requires physical action and the other does not. As previously noted, merely stating that one is an evangelical does not generate the same type of outcomes as attending a house of worship on a regular basis. Saying "I'm a Muslim" is not at all the same as going to the local mosque each week or saying prayers five times a day. In fact, as we will discuss in more detail later, a tremendous amount of social science research points to a variety of positive benefits of religious behavior, while the literature is not so clear about the net gain of mere religious belonging.

When we look at the data, though, a clear narrative begins to emerge: Of the three B's, religious behavior has seen the most significant decline over the last fifty years. The General Social Survey has been asking about a respondent's religious affiliation and attendance since 1972, and it added a question about religious belief in 1988. I calculated the share of the sample that claimed no religious affiliation, the percentage of respondents who never attended religious services, and the percentage of people who

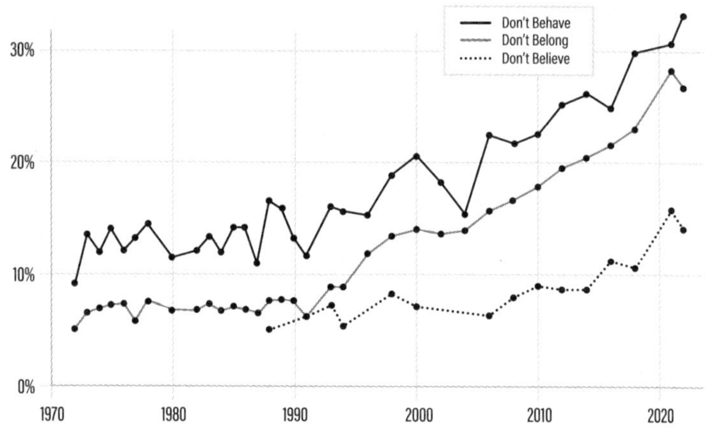

Figure 8.1 Belief, behavior, and belonging in American religion, 1972–2022

indicated that they were either atheist or agnostic. I then tracked those trend lines over the last several decades (see fig. 8.1).

In the early 1970s, the share of Americans who never attended religious services and claimed no religious affiliation was incredibly low. Just about 5 percent were religiously unaffiliated, and 9 percent indicated that they never darkened the door of a church. For the next two decades, those lines were remarkably flat. Even into the early 1990s, the portion of the sample who never attended a religious service hovered between 11 and 14 percent, and the nones in the sample never got above 6 percent. When the question about religious belief was added to the survey in 1988, just one in twenty respondents had an atheist or agnostic view of God. But the next several decades would put those three trend lines on slightly different trajectories.

The proportion of the sample who didn't engage in religious behavior rose significantly between 1992 and 2022. By the late 2000s, the share of Americans who were never-attenders was clearly above 20 percent, and it continued to increase from there. In the most recent survey collected in 2022, about a third of folks were never-attenders. As has been previously described, the nones' percentage rose consistently for decades as well. It was north of 20 percent by the mid-2010s and in the most recent sample was about 28 percent of all American adults. But that is still about five points lower than the share of never-attenders. The proportion of those in the sample who don't believe in God has never been that high and even into 2014 was less than 10 percent of adults. In the last several years, it has crept up though. In both 2016 and 2018, it was slightly more than 10 percent, and in the last two surveys collected in 2021 and 2022, the percentage of people with atheist or agnostic views hovered around 15 percent.

One of my pet peeves when talking with academics is that they always have to give highly nuanced answers to what are often fairly straightforward questions. In this case, it's "How religious is the average American?" As can be clearly seen from the previous data analysis, the answer is highly dependent on how one conceptualizes religion. If the question is oriented to more visible measures of religiosity, like church attendance, the answer is a significant portion of Americans are not religious at all. The same can largely be said when answering the question through the lens of religious belonging: Nearly three in ten adults indicate that they have no religious affiliation. But when 85 percent of survey respondents say they believe in God or a higher power, even with some doubts, that conjures a much different portrait of the American religious landscape. Even as religious behavior and belonging have fallen by the wayside for tens of millions, religious belief is still incredibly robust.

Many Americans obviously live between the two poles of being entirely religious and not being religious at all. Belief in God is pervasive, but religious attendance is scarcer in the adult population. To get a sense of just how many people live at each edge of the religiosity continuum, I generated two measures. One is people who are religious in all three dimensions—they claim a religious affiliation, they attend religious services nearly every week or more, and they indicate that they have a certain belief in God. The other measure is those who are not religious in all three dimensions—they never attend religious services, they claim no religious affiliation, and they express an atheist or agnostic view of God. I then tracked the size of these two groups over the last thirty-five years (see fig. 8.2).

What may come as a surprise is that the percentage of Americans who were religious in all three dimensions was never that large during the period examined. In 1988, about 30 percent of people in the General Social Survey were regular attendees of a house of worship, had a certain belief in God, and had a religious affiliation. The idea that a large portion of the general public was very religious is demonstrably false when the data is looked at through this simple metric. It's true that many people are religious on one measure, or maybe even two, but the number of Americans who

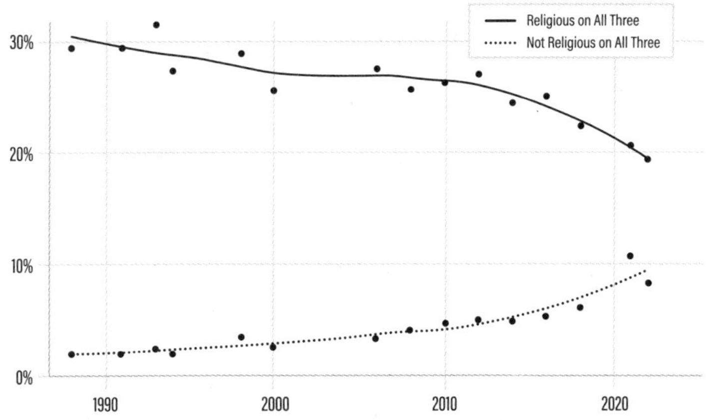

Figure 8.2 Shares of the population that are completely religious and completely nonreligious, 1988–2022

are religious on belief, behavior, and belonging measures has never been that large. That number has also been dropping slowly over time. By the early 2010s, the share who were religious across all three dimensions dipped below 25 percent, and it has continued to slide from there. In the latest surveys, about one in five adults was religious on all three metrics.

But the other side of the coin is the portion of the sample that was not religious on any of the three measures. That group was vanishingly small back in the late 1980s—just about 2 percent of the sample never attended religious services, claimed no religious affiliation, and said that God didn't exist or that it was impossible to know whether God existed. It is also striking how slowly this percentage has risen over the decades. As recently as 2016, the portion of the sample that was nonreligious on all three metrics was about 5 percent. Said another way, in 2016, 95 percent of Americans were at least somewhat religious. In the last couple years, though, the number of nones has jumped considerably. It's fair to say that the none-none-none percentage of Americans is likely about 10 percent.

But what may be even more revealing is the line that doesn't appear in figure 8.2: Those who are religious in at least one dimension. In 1988, 30 percent of the sample was in the top trend line—religious on all three dimensions—while about 2 percent were not religious at all. That means over two-thirds of the sample was religious in one or two dimensions. They may have had a certain belief in God but never attended religious services, or they may have belonged to the Latter-day Saints and attended religious services nearly every week but didn't have a certain belief in God. There are literally thousands of ways to explain the people who existed between the top and bottom lines of this graph. What may be even more fascinating is that as these two trend lines began to move closer to each other over time, they still amounted to essentially the same percentage: About 30 percent of the sample was completely religious or not religious at all.

In other words, the portion of adults who were between the two poles was largely unchanged over the last thirty-five years. In the United States, about seven in ten people are "kind of" religious. They either believe in God, affiliate with a religious tradition, or attend religious services at least a little bit. Or they may do two of these things. But they are neither all the way in nor all the way out of religion, based on these three metrics.

The Faithful Versus the Faithless?

Yet, although most people are at least a bit religious according to one of these dimensions, a worrying trend has emerged in the data regarding how some people seem to understand what religion means in their lives. For a small portion of Americans (20 percent according to the data from fig. 8.2), religion is an all-consuming part of their lives. They attend religious services at their house of worship and study the sacred text of their faith to try to live better, more fulfilling lives. They believe God helps them through the most difficult moments and gives them guidance to navigate life's complexities. These are people who possess a religious worldview, and their actions portray their inward orientation toward matters of faith. They don't just say religion is important to them; they act based on that belief.

However, for an increasing number of Americans, religion seems to operate as little more than a tribal identity. When they say that they are Christians, they are not necessarily expressing a commitment to the gospel of Jesus Christ. Instead, it's a way to say what kind of values they stand for, what causes they support, and what candidates they vote for on Election Day. It provides a justification for their worldview; it is not their worldview. As has been previously discussed, the growing consensus in the academic literature is that religion now exists downstream of politics. Instead of using a theological framework to justify a voting decision, individuals use their partisanship to determine who will receive their support and then find a biblical justification for making such a choice. In essence, this reduces religion to its worst, most caustic aspects. This understanding of what religion is creates "us versus them" and appeals to divine authority in a post hoc way.

A series of questions in many large surveys help illustrate this. One is quite simple: "How important is religion to your life?" Four possible responses range from "very important" to "not at all important." This question is incredibly illuminating because of its vagueness. It's not a concrete query like "How often do you attend religious services?" or "What is your present religion?" Instead, it probes the amorphous idea of the respondent's general orientation toward religion. If someone says religion is very important to their life, that doesn't necessarily mean they are a churchgoing person; it just indicates that they think religion should play a central role in their life. One would assume that questions of religious importance and religious attendance would run on the same tracks and that people who attend more frequently would be more likely to say that religion is important and vice versa. And that's generally the case when one analyzes the entire sample. However, once the sample is broken down into Democrats and Republicans, a much different pattern emerges.

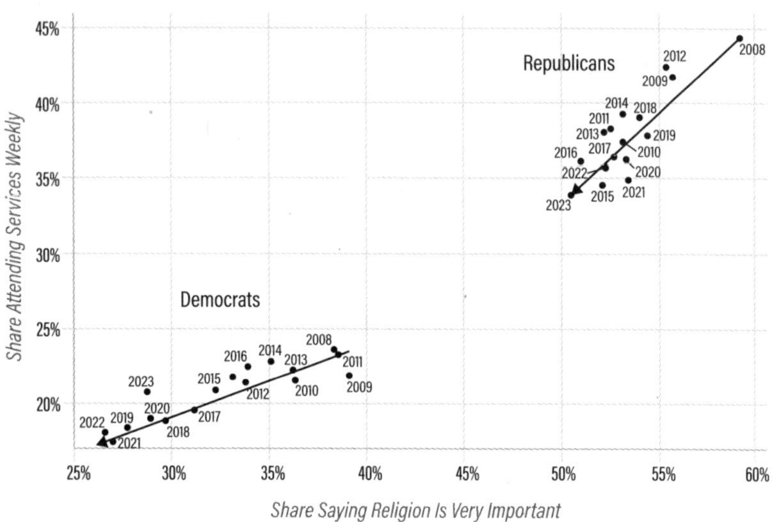

Figure 8.3 Religion's importance and religious attendance among Democrats and Republicans, 2008–23

In figure 8.3, Democrats clearly score lower than Republicans on measures of religious attendance and religious importance. For instance, in 2008 about 38 percent of Democrats said that religion was very important, and 24 percent reported that they attended religious services weekly. Among Republicans that same year, 59 percent said that religion was very important, and 44 percent indicated weekly attendance. But when data from the next fifteen years is plotted, the trajectory of the two groups varies significantly and tells an important story about how religion is understood through the lens of politics in the twenty-first century.

For Democrats, the movement on religious importance is much larger than the shift on religious attendance. The share of Democrats who said that religion was very important went from 38 percent in 2008 to just 27 percent in 2022. Meanwhile, the drop in weekly attendance among Democrats was much smaller—23 to 18 percent during that same period. Religious importance was down by eleven points, while attendance was down by five points. Among

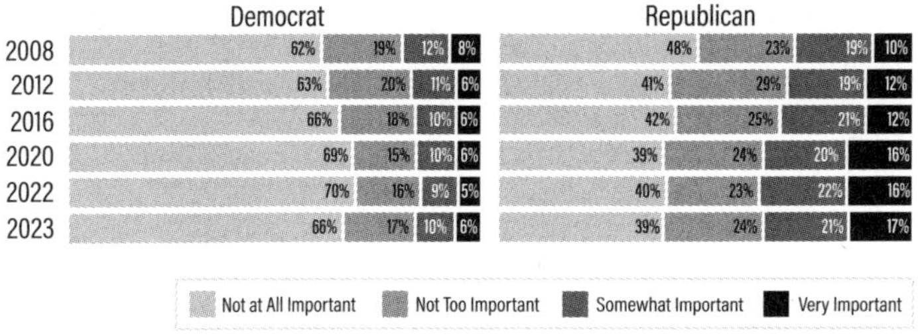

Figure 8.4 Religious importance among never-attending Democrats and Republicans, 2008–23

Republicans, it's a much different portrait. Religious importance was 59 percent in 2008, and it dropped to about 51 percent in the latest surveys—a decline of eight points. However, religious attendance dropped more. Among Republicans in 2008, 44 percent reported weekly attendance. In 2023, that number was 34 percent. Think of it this way: For Democrats, the numerical difference between importance and attendance is nine percentage points (27 versus 18 percent). For Republicans, that gap is 17 points (51 versus 34 percent). It seems to be an emerging trend that a significant number of Republicans believe that religion is very important but don't attend religious services on a regular basis. Democrats are leaving behind both aspects of religion in a more linear fashion.

This comes into sharper focus in figure 8.4, which restricts the sample to those who never attend religious services and shows responses to the question about religious importance for both Democrats and Republicans over the last several years. Among Democrats, a significant majority of those who never attend religious services said religion was "not at all important." Since 2016, at least two-thirds of the sample has fit into this category, and another 15–20 percent has said that it's "not too important." That means just 15 percent of Democrats who never attend religious services said that religion was "somewhat important" or "very important." It's also worth pointing out that the trend line over time is in the direction of lower religious importance for never-attending Democrats, with the 2023 numbers standing as an outlier.

Among Republicans, the picture is much different. In every year of the survey, among Republicans who never attend religious services, a majority still said that religion was important. In fact, the share of Republicans who chose the "not important at all" option has declined over time. In the 2022 sample, about 40 percent of never-attending Republicans said that religion was "not important at all." That's thirty percentage points lower than for Democrats who never attend religious services. What is truly remarkable is the share of Republicans who said that religion was "somewhat important" or "very important" to them. In the 2008 sample, it was 29 percent of never-attenders. In the most recent samples from 2022 and 2023, that percentage rose to 38 percent. Even as the share of Republicans who never attend religious services has increased from 10 percent in 2008 to 22 percent in 2023, their belief that religion is important has increased.

This result speaks to the convergence of at least two trends in American religion and society over the last five decades. The first was already discussed in chapter 5, the rising secularization in American society. The proportion of nonreligious respondents has gone from 5 percent around 1990 to nearly 30 percent in more recent data. A group doesn't get that large without drawing in people from every facet of American life. The other phenomenon at play here is the growing God gap between the two major parties. It's clear from the data that Democrats have benefited more from the growth of the nones, but there are also more and more Republicans who are walking away from certain aspects of religious life. While their attendance may be waning, they are still attached to the idea of religion. They like that religion speaks to things like family values and traditional beliefs on gender, sexuality, and abortion.

Thus, while Democrats haven't left religion behind entirely, they aren't believing, behaving, or belonging at nearly the rate they were several decades ago. Republicans have been walking away in a more uneven manner. Religious attendance is down, for instance, but very few Republicans will call themselves atheists or agnostics or declare that they don't believe in God. They appreciate the cultural aspects of religion, even if they aren't engaging in regular worship activities or weekly Bible studies. In essence, they like the idea of religion without the actual religious practice part. Being opposed to abortion is now a political stance with a religious justification, not a theological posture that expresses itself in how one votes on Election Day. For many Americans who are turned off by the increasingly polarized nature of politics, religion has become another way to drive a wedge in the electorate. It's the faithful versus the faithless.

The Rise of the Nonchurchgoing Evangelical

There's other evidence that terms traditionally seen as describing a religious commitment have become more about politics than theology. Take, for instance, the simple term "evangelical." The term's etymology is undisputed; it comes from the Greek word *euangelion*, which means "gospel" or "good news." The famous religious historian George Marsden once noted that in the 1950s and 1960s, the definition of evangelical was simple—anyone who liked Billy Graham. For much of the twentieth century, an evangelical was seen as someone who took the Bible seriously and tried to lead other people into a salvific understanding of the death and resurrection of Jesus Christ.

Yet several insights emerging in survey data suggest that the term "evangelical" is becoming unmoored from its religious roots.

For the last twenty years or so, most public opinion surveys have included a simple yes or no question: "Do you consider yourself a born-again or evangelical Christian, or not?" This simple act of self-identification offers a tremendous amount of insight. For instance, it's been the widely held view among scholars and the general public alike that evangelicals are in church on a regular

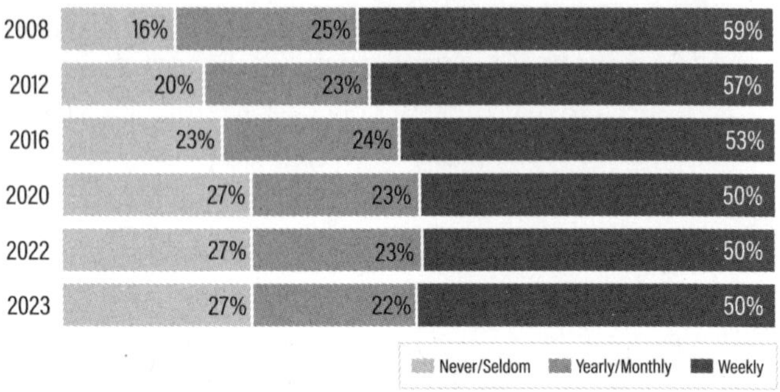

Figure 8.5 Religious attendance among self-identified evangelicals, 2008–23

basis because they take their faith very seriously. But if one looks at the church attendance of individuals who self-identify as evangelical over the last fifteen years, that conception of highly active evangelicals becomes a bit more complicated (see fig. 8.5). In 2008, nearly 60 percent of evangelicals attended worship services at least once a week, and only 16 percent said that their attendance was seldom or never. But in the intervening years, those numbers have begun to shift in notable ways. By 2020, the share of evangelicals who were weekly attenders had dropped by nearly ten percentage points to just 50 percent. At the same time, the share who attended religious services less than once a year had increased to 27 percent.

Some people will read the previous paragraph and have an immediate, almost visceral reaction. "It's not possible to be an evangelical who doesn't go to church." This is, of course, not true by empirical standards. When people taking a survey are asked a question, they get to provide whatever answer comes to mind. If they feel like the term "evangelical" describes them well, they are allowed to indicate that. No one gets to own a word—its meaning comes from how it's used in modern parlance. For a growing number of Americans, there's no incongruence between identifying as evangelical and not attending church.

Anyone who has worked with surveys knows that there's always the possibility of survey error. That's the idea that people simply make mistakes when they provide their responses. They may not read a question correctly, or they may check the wrong box when entering their response. There are many ways in which one's views could be wrongly recorded. But there's a simple way to check for survey error—in this case, seeing whether there is a theoretical justification for why someone would report both that they are an evangelical and that they never attend religious services. One likely explanation for this is clearly political partisanship. Given the aforementioned God gap, it may be the case that Republicans are seeing a religious term as also encompassing a political orientation. Several trends in the data support this conclusion.

Given that evangelicalism is related to religious devotion, it makes sense that when Protestants attend church at a high frequency, they are more likely to self-identify as evangelical. That's clearly the case when looking at the data (see fig. 8.6). Among

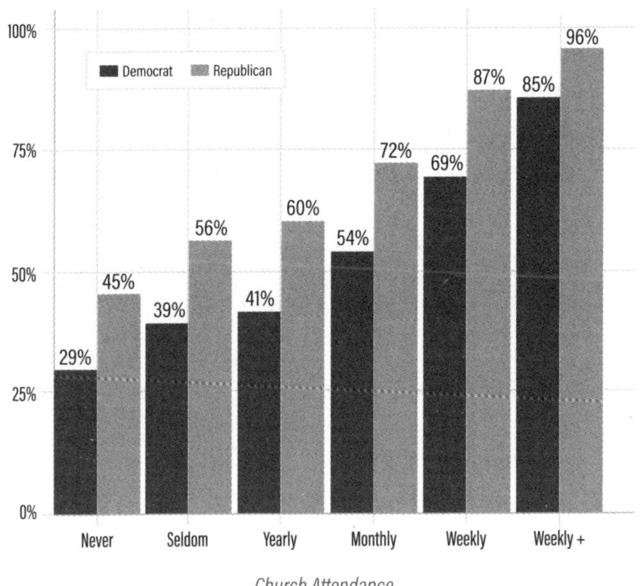

Figure 8.6 Share of Protestants who identify as born-again/evangelical by church attendance and party affiliation, 2020–23

Protestants who never attend religious services, just 40 percent self-identified as evangelical, but every step up the attendance ladder leads to that percentage growing. Fifty-three percent of yearly attenders, 65 percent of those who go monthly, 81 percent of weekly attenders, and nearly all of those who attend church multiple times a week self-identified as evangelical (88 percent).

However, when the sample is divided into Democrats and Republicans, a huge partisan gap emerges. For instance, not quite half of Republican Protestants who never go to church said that they were evangelical (45 percent). Only 29 percent of Democrats were in this nonattending category. There is an increase in evangelical identification among both Democrats and Republicans as church attendance becomes more frequent, but the pew gap persists at each level. In most categories, it's a nearly twenty-point gap in evangelical affiliation between Democrats and Republicans. Among Democrat Protestants who attend church once a week, 69 percent said that they were evangelical versus 87 percent of Republicans. This is pretty compelling evidence that church attendance, when combined with Republican affiliation, correlates with much higher levels of evangelical identification than it does when combined with Democratic affiliation.

However, one of the interesting things about many modern datasets is that this evangelical self-identification question is asked to every respondent whether they indicate that they are a Protestant, Catholic, Muslim, or atheist. It may seem a bit odd that a Jew is asked if they are a born-again or evangelical Christian or not. Any cursory understanding of Judaism and evangelical theology would indicate that these two religious identities are completely incompatible. For those taking the survey who are non-Christians, it would be easy enough to say that they are not evangelical and move on to the next section. But a surprising number of non-Protestants indicate that they are, in fact, evangelical.

It is logical that a significant portion of Protestants say that they are evangelical—about 60 percent in many surveys. There

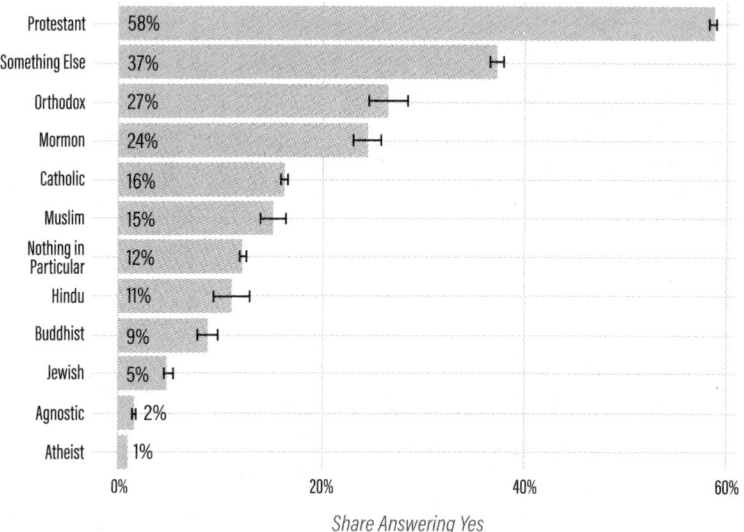

Figure 8.7 Share of the population that identifies as born-again/evangelical by religious tradition, 2020–23

are other religious respondents among whom a significant portion say that they are evangelical, including Orthodox Christians (27 percent), Latter-day Saints (24 percent), and Catholics (16 percent). But then there are a number of faiths that have almost nothing in common with evangelicalism, yet a significant number of their adherents say that they are born-again (see fig. 8.7). Among Muslims in the sample, 15 percent said that they were born-again or evangelical, followed by 11 percent of Hindus, 9 percent of Buddhists, and 5 percent of Jews. Again, this could very easily be chalked up to people taking the survey in a haphazard manner. They merely click buttons as fast as they can to get to the end and receive their compensation for completing the instrument. This is a common problem in survey research, and while there are ways to mitigate this concern, it's impossible to entirely eliminate these lower quality responses. However, one way to determine whether something is truly a survey error is to see whether that possible error is randomly distributed throughout the sample. There can

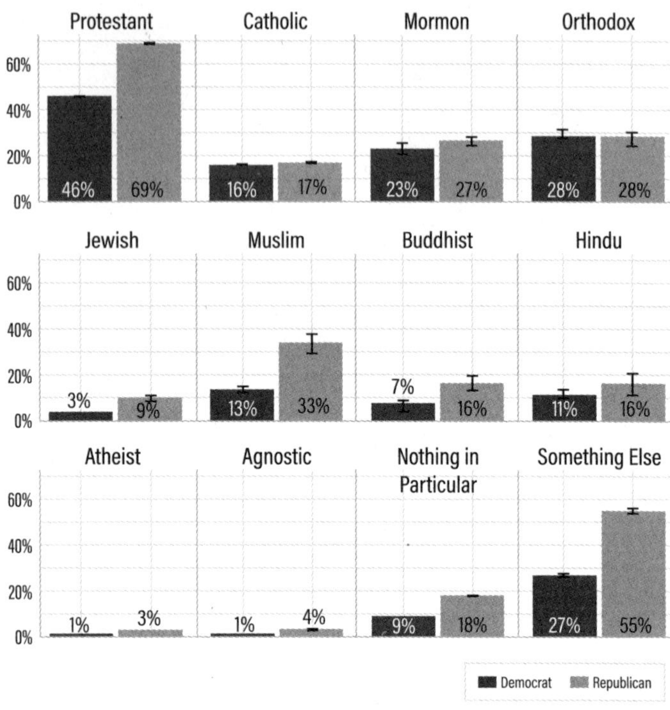

Figure 8.8 Share of the population that identifies as born-again/evangelical by religious tradition and party affiliation, 2020–23

be no coherent theory as to why respondents would say that they are evangelical Muslims in this case. But, as previously mentioned, there is a testable hypothesis here: Republicans are more likely to self-identify as evangelical than Democrats, regardless of their stated religious affiliation.

When the sample is divided into a dozen religious groups and then separated into Democrats and Republicans, the nature of evangelical self-identification comes into much sharper focus (see fig. 8.8). Among Republican Protestants, about 70 percent self-identified as evangelical, whereas just 46 percent of Protestant Democrats did so. That makes sense based on previous analysis. Among the other three Christian groups across the top of this graph, the differences between evangelical self-identification are small when comparing Democrats with Republicans. However, in the second row of non-Christian groups, a clear pattern emerges. About 9 percent of Republican Jews said that they were evangelical compared with 3 percent of Democratic Jews. Among Muslims, a third of Republicans were evangelical compared with 13 percent of Democrats. There's a nine-point partisan gap in identification among Buddhists and a five-point difference among Hindus. A Republican who described their religion as "nothing in particular" was twice as likely to say they were evangelical than a Democrat with the same religious identification.

In all twelve religious classifications, there's not a single instance in which Democrats were more likely to identify as evangelical compared with Republicans. That's true among Protestants, but it's also apparent among Jews, Muslims, and Buddhists. It's incredibly unlikely that random survey errors would result in such a consistent partisan gap across multiple datasets and a dozen religious traditions. The more likely and most defensible explanation is the simplest one: The word "evangelical" has become a shorthand for people of all faith groups to say, "I'm a political conservative." It's no longer primarily a theological belief in the death and resurrection of Jesus Christ. For a growing number of Americans, to be an evangelical is to vote for Republicans on Election Day.

Is Religion Another Source of Division?

Despite the efforts of preachers and rank-and-file evangelicals, the average American increasingly understands religion through the lens of tribalism. It's a way to say which political team one plays for, whom they find common cause with, and how they line up during an election season. When this is understood, it makes more sense why religion is declining in the United States. As previously mentioned, the most empirically beneficial aspect of religion—regularly attending worship—has declined rapidly. At the same time, the most divisive and caustic aspect of religion—the belonging component—has moved to center stage. Given that polarization has ripped through the country over the last several decades, it logically follows that the average person would use religion to determine whether someone shares their political viewpoint. Rather than helping people build bridges to others who are slightly different from them, religion has become just one more means we use to sort ourselves into groups.

Maybe one of the reasons religion has declined significantly is because of the way it's being understood in public discourse. If religion is a marker of which political tribe one belongs to or how one views cultural issues, that may be more than enough reason for many to want nothing to do with a faith community. What exacerbates this is the sense that there's one way to be a white Christian in the United States: the conservative way. The idea that there are politically diverse churches or even left-of-center houses of worship is foreign to a lot of young people. We should remember that Generation Z came of age when the mainline was largely irrelevant numerically and white evangelicals were lining up behind the GOP. Thus, they may be repulsed not by religion but by what religion has become: another way to keep the country polarized.

Of course, there is no easy solution to the problem of "religious in name only." Probably the best thing people of faith can do is make sure that they don't lead with or emphasize the political ramifications of their religious affiliation. Noting that one's church runs an effective clothing ministry or does a great job of tutoring students in an afterschool program reminds others that houses of worship aren't just weekly Republican Party meetings. As previously mentioned, it seems that younger people are increasingly blank slates when it comes to their understanding of what religious groups do and do not do. Even in environments where politics and religion are highly divisive, people tend to admire others—even those they disagree with on some political issues—who are truly driven by their faith to live lives of character, integrity, and service.

PART 3

A WAY FORWARD

9

How Polarized Are We, Really?

THE BIG TAKEAWAYS

- The loudest voices on social media often tout the most extreme views. But they don't represent the average American.
- A closer look at the data reveals that the typical American (religious or not) tends to be moderate, sensible, and pragmatic when faced with contentious issues of the day.

When I was in graduate school, my concentration was in American politics. I didn't know it when I enrolled, but at the time my chosen field was being roiled by an intense debate over the question "Are we actually polarized?" I know that seems like an incredibly easy question to answer given the evidence presented in this book. Based on all the charts and graphs on the previous pages, it seems that the answer to this question is yes, absolutely.

But what if the answer isn't so straightforward?

That was the primary disagreement in the academic literature that I was reading as part of my coursework. Two camps formed around this issue. One side made a strong argument that what was happening should be described as "elite polarization." Simply put, it wasn't the rank-and-file voters who were being pulled to the extremes of the ideological spectrum. Rather, it was the donors, media elites, and politicians who were using divisive rhetoric to advance their causes in the halls of power. This school of thought believed that things like gerrymandering were eradicating "purple districts," where Democrats and Republicans could be found in fairly equal proportions. Congressional districts were being drawn in ways that ensured that the only elections that actually mattered were the party primaries, where Democrats (or Republicans) selected nominees who would win the general elections in statistical landslides. Because primary voters tend to be highly engaged citizens who lean toward ideologues, focusing on the edges of the political spectrum was the only way to ensure victory.

The other camp argued that polarization wasn't relegated to just the upper crust of American society. They contended that it had seeped into the rank-and-file voters (and churchgoers), who populate small towns and big cities across the United States. Anyone who spends time on social media has seen firsthand evidence of this type of polarization. The comments section of a Facebook community group is often filled with hateful and unhinged conspiracy theories and poisonous vitriol pointed toward people on the other side of the aisle. Many everyday Americans feel they can't talk about politics at Thanksgiving or Christmas gatherings because the conversation will end up in raised voices and hurt feelings. This understanding of mass polarization just "feels" right to us as we navigate our everyday lives.

So, which one is correct? As most things are in the academic world, the answer is, "It's complicated."

Political commentator Ezra Klein published a book called *Why We're Polarized*, in which he takes a middle path on this debate.[1]

Klein is certainly convinced that there has been near-complete elite polarization in this country, but he believes that over the last few decades the two parties have staked out clearly distinct ideological positions, which in turn has led to increased sorting among the rank and file. This is exacerbated by the nature of American politics, which really allows for the existence of only two parties. Voters feel as though they must pick a side and then feel forced to at least feign beliefs that align with the orthodoxy of their political party.

I think that is exactly the case in American religious institutions as well—and the data backs up this assertion. Yes, white evangelicals are more likely today to identify as Republicans and conservatives than they were twenty years ago, and atheists are more likely to see themselves to the left side of the political spectrum. But does that mean they actually agree with their respective parties on an entire range of issues? A raft of polling data says they do not. In fact, average Americans are often much more pragmatic, sensible, and open-minded than they are given credit for. In other words, the average American doesn't want to be polarized but feels they must be if they want to fit into the religious and political landscape of the United States.

The Overlooked Moderate

Since 1988, the General Social Survey has regularly asked respondents whether they have ever had a "born-again" experience. They also ask people to report their religious affiliation. What fascinates me is the number of Americans who indicate that they have never been born-again, but neither do they align with the nonreligious. In other words, they are the overlooked Americans who stand in the middle between evangelicals on one side and the nones on the other (see fig. 9.1).

The question about born-again status was first asked in 1988 and again in 1991. In both of those years, nearly 60 percent of

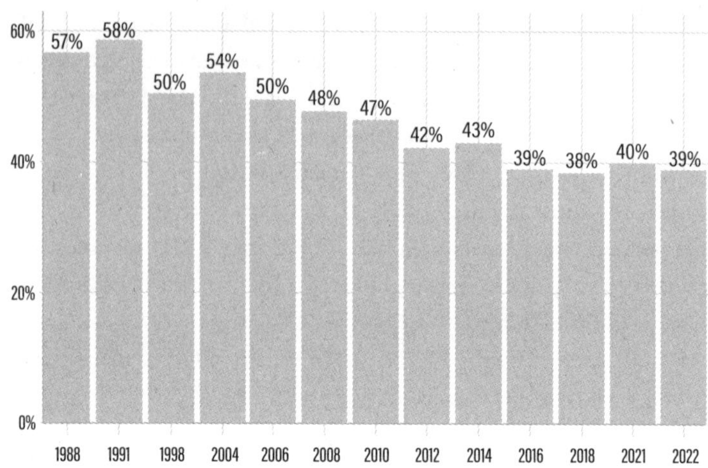

Figure 9.1 Share of the population that was never born-again and is not nones, 1988–2022

Americans had never had a born-again experience but still identified with a religious tradition—mainline Protestants and Catholics made up the bulk of this group. But over time, that group eroded. By 2006, only about half of respondents fell into that camp; the rest either claimed no religious affiliation or said they had had a born-again experience. In surveys collected between 2016 and 2022, the share of Americans in the "middle"—some religious affiliation but not born-again—had dropped to just 40 percent, a nearly twenty-point decline in three decades.

Of course, a big reason for this is the rising number of Americans who claim no religious affiliation—that rose from 5 percent in the early 1990s to about 28 percent in the most recent surveys. But another underdiscussed reason is the fact that the share of Americans who have had born-again experiences has actually increased somewhat over the last thirty years. In 1988, the share of the sample that had been born-again was about 36 percent. In 2018, that percentage had increased to 41 percent. The middle is being chipped away by both the left and the right sides of the religious spectrum. While about two in five Americans have managed to resist the pull to either side, that share is significantly smaller (and quite a bit less vocal) today than it was thirty or forty years ago.

I have a friend in academia who got a job as a research assistant on a grant-funded project that tried to understand the motivations of mainline Protestants. One aspect of the research design was a series of focus groups with United Methodists, Episcopalians, and members of other traditionally moderate denominations. (Remember from chapter 3 that the mainline is more moderate than common perception suggests.) My friend led a focus group through a series of questions and prompts about their levels of political engagement. Most reported paying attention to political events on a daily basis. The vast majority said that they voted in presidential elections, and many of them reported that they also voted in midterm races and local contests. In other words, these folks were pretty active politically. Then she asked them when they last attended a political protest. The room went dead silent. Eventually, a sweet older woman looked at my friend and said in a soothing voice, "Honey, moderates don't march."

Back in 2010, comedians Jon Stewart and Stephen Colbert organized an event in Washington, DC, called "Rally to Restore Sanity and/or Fear." It was basically a spoof of a traditional protest march that tried to get middle-of-the-road, pragmatic voters off their couches and into the fray. The signs that people designed for the event told the whole story:

> "I respectfully disagree with your opinions but I still value you as a person."
>
> "Signs are an impractical medium for civil discourse."
>
> "I support reasonable conclusions based on supported facts."
>
> "Civil is sexy."[2]

The average American is much more aligned with the sentiments expressed by those signs than they are with the type of person who attends a typical rally in the nation's capital. Yet they are nearly nonexistent on cable news channels and social media apps.

Contradictory Views on "Simple" Issues

The University of Notre Dame published a research report in 2020 organized by the McGrath Institute for Church Life titled "How Americans Understand Abortion."[3] Led by Tricia Bruce, the research included 217 in-depth interviews with people from all walks of life from six states scattered across the country. This research makes it plain that the vast majority of Americans have highly nuanced and often contradictory views on some of the most contentious issues in religion and politics.

One of the major findings was that most interview subjects were incredibly reluctant to talk about abortion, knowing it could stir up conflict. Many also said that they try their best to avoid judging other people when the topic comes up. But that stance often conflicted with their moral convictions: Some viewed abortion as unequivocally wrong yet simultaneously claimed they didn't want to judge those who supported it or had undergone the procedure. The result is a quiet tension: They hold strong beliefs but hesitate to express them, fearing interpersonal fallout. Another conclusion from these interviews was that surveys tend to oversimplify how Americans view abortion. Bruce writes, "Many interviewees gave us an initial answer to a survey-style question before disclosing that's not really how they feel." The report notes that most people "do not hold bipolar views toward abortion but multidimensional ones." In other words, they waffle, they equivocate, they include caveats and scenarios that could change their position on whether a woman should have the right to choose an abortion.

In total, of the 217 people surveyed, 75 said abortion should be "legal under any circumstance." But even among those who favored permitting abortion in any situation, about half of them expressed a moral ambivalence toward abortion or outright moral opposition. An overwhelming sense from the interview subjects was that abortion is a "tough subject" that has a lot of "gray area" involved. One of the most compelling conclusions from this research effort was that "none of the Americans we interviewed talked about abortion as a desirable good." The interview subjects, even those who labeled themselves pro-choice, were quick to mention that the decision to end a pregnancy is hard and should be taken seriously. Hesitation and doubt exist even among people on the extremes of this debate.

Even though survey measurement is often an imprecise gauge of what people are thinking and feeling about a topic as complex as abortion, there are times when quantitative data can tell a compelling story. For instance, in this study, respondents were asked to place themselves on a scale that ran from 1 (pro-choice) to 10 (pro-life). In figure 9.2, we see that just 18 percent of respondents placed themselves as far to the left as possible, and nearly

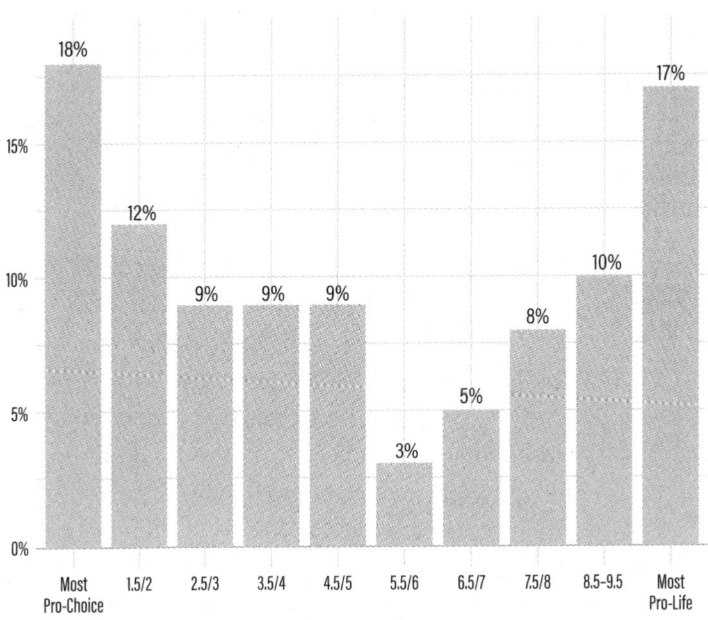

Figure 9.2 Scale from most pro-choice to most pro-life, 2020

the same percentage put themselves on the far right of the scale. In numerical terms, if we put six random people in a room and asked them about abortion, one of them would be as far right as possible, and one would be as far left as possible. But that means that four of those six people would be somewhere in between. Yet only the two people on the poles are typically asked to represent the whole abortion debate in popular media; only their tweets get the most engagement.

The binary nature of American politics (Republican versus Democrat) belies the reality that average Americans don't completely agree with the stated positions of either party. We've all seen the bumper sticker turned social meme that includes the text, "The Bible says it. I believe it. That settles it." In fact, many religious Americans who are familiar with biblical texts and take their faith seriously just can't arrive at such simple conclusions. They want life to be black and white, but their lived experience tells them that there are few situations that are so cut and dried. Barack Obama said that religion is best when it comes with a healthy dose of doubt.[4] That tends to be the posture that the majority of Americans take on matters of morality.

Ambivalent Evangelicals

The perception of American religious groups, especially evangelicalism, is that the pews are packed each Sunday with "true believers"—people who believe that the Bible is the literal Word of God and that Jesus Christ is the only way to salvation. This is likely perpetuated by snippets of sermons that people have seen or heard in which a man stands behind the pulpit imploring the congregation to get right with Jesus or risk spending eternity in torment. Yet when actual evangelicals are asked about so-called black-and-white issues in religion, what emerges is a lot of ambivalence and little unanimity on some of the pressing issues in theology.

Over the past decade, Ligonier Ministries has conducted a regular survey of the American public called the State of Theology. The research team compiles a sample of the general population as well as an oversample (a poll of a specific group to better understand their views and behaviors) of people who could be described as evangelical based on a four-statement criteria. Those four statements of faith emphasize the importance of the Bible, the need for evangelizing the lost, the salvific nature of Jesus's death on the cross, and a belief that only those who trust in Jesus will obtain salvation. In other words, these evangelicals are not the type who just self-identify as evangelical. They fit fairly restrictive criteria when it comes to their religious beliefs and behaviors. What is especially striking is that the State of Theology reveals an evangelicalism that is much less dogmatic than popular perceptions of evangelicals.

For instance, the survey poses this statement to evangelicals: "God accepts the worship of all religions, including Christianity, Judaism, and Islam." This statement seems to stand in direct opposition to Jesus's words in the Gospel of John: "I am the way and the truth and the life. No one comes to the Father except through me" (14:6). Despite this seeming clarity from Scripture, a significant portion of evangelicals believe that God accepts the worship of Muslims and Jews. In 2016, a larger portion of evangelicals agreed with that statement than disagreed with it (49 versus 43 percent) (see fig. 9.3). In fact, in the last four times this survey has

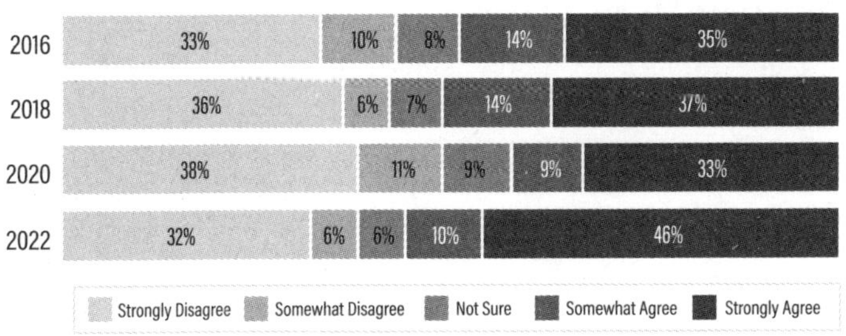

Figure 9.3 Evangelicals' responses to the statement "God accepts the worship of all religions, including Christianity, Judaism, and Islam," 2016–22

been fielded, a majority of evangelicals never disagreed with this statement. In the last several years, a simple majority believed that God accepts worship from other faith traditions. In the most recent data collected in 2022, that figure stood at 56 percent—the highest on record. This analysis does not conclude that evangelicals have an exclusivist orientation toward God. In fact, the conclusion is just the opposite: Most of them believe that God is just as attentive to Muslims' worship as to that of Southern Baptists or Roman Catholics.

Other responses suggest that evangelicals tend to take a fairly moderate stance on what is perceived as core tenets of their theology. Another statement in the State of Theology survey is, "Jesus was a great teacher, but he was not God." In 2020, when this statement was first included, two-thirds of evangelicals disagreed with it, while about three in ten agreed (see fig. 9.4). But when that same statement was posed to evangelicals in 2022, the results looked much different: 43 percent of evangelical Christians agreed that Jesus was not God, while only 54 percent disagreed. Remember, these were not merely self-identified evangelicals. Instead, these were people who had to conform to a definition of evangelicalism that was based on a four-question typology regarding their beliefs about the Bible, salvation, and the need to evangelize. Yet, even among people who met these qualifications, there was still a significant majority that was less than certain about key theological issues.

We can see this moderate, pragmatic stance in other data as well. In 2018, the Public Religion Research Institute collaborated with *The Atlantic* to survey Americans on how they felt about

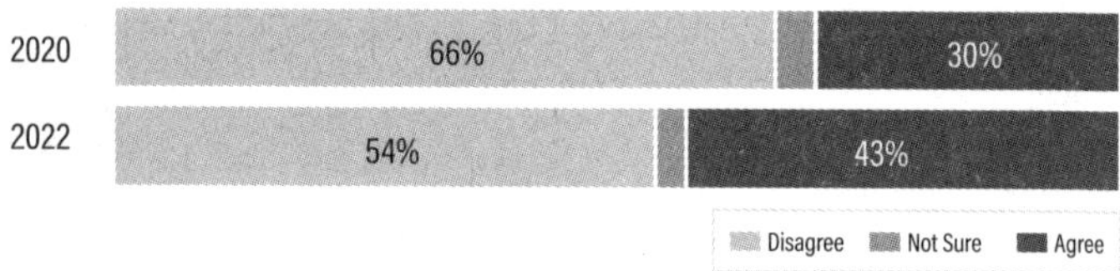

Figure 9.4 Evangelicals' responses to the statement "Jesus was a great teacher, but he was not God," 2020–22

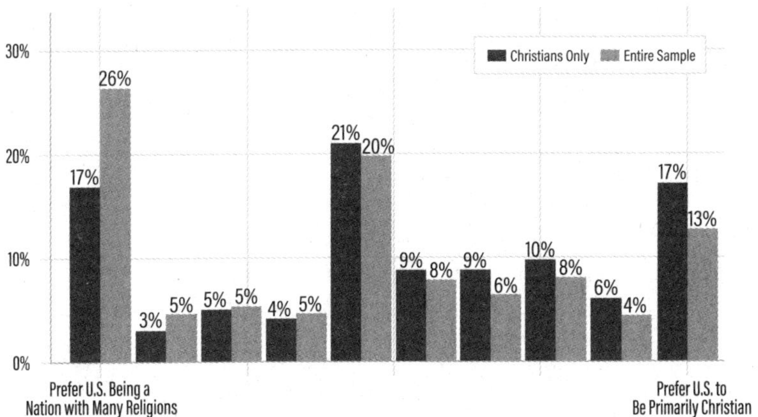

Figure 9.5 The preferred religious composition of the United States among Christians and the general population, 2018

issues like religious pluralism. For instance, respondents were asked to think about their ideal religious composition for the country. They were given a range in which 1 meant "I would prefer the US to be a nation made up of people belonging to a wide variety of religious beliefs" and 10 meant "I would prefer the US to be a nation primarily made up of people who follow the Christian faith." I calculated the distribution of responses to this question for the entire sample and then just for people who identified with a Christian tradition (see fig. 9.5).

What is striking to me is how little the responses differ between the two samples. One would assume that Christians would have a strong preference for a country that was primarily Christian, but that's not actually the case. Instead, just 17 percent of Christians said that they would strongly prefer a United States that was Christian. That was just four percentage points higher than the entire sample. On this scale that ranged from 1 to 10, the share of Christians who chose an answer of at least 6 was just half the sample. That means that exactly half the sample of Christians would prefer a country that had much more religious diversity. This data refutes the idea that there's a huge contingent of American

Christians who are being driven to religiously purify the country and make sure it is primarily Christian. Of course, such people do exist. About a third of the Christian sample chose an 8 or higher, but they certainly do not represent the majority position among Christians in the United States.

Also in the same survey, Christians were asked whether they would be happy or unhappy if their child married a person of a different religious faith. Just a quarter said that they would be "somewhat unhappy" or "very unhappy." The most popular answer by a significant margin was "neither happy nor unhappy," chosen by 55 percent of Christians taking the survey. When the entire sample was asked whether religious organizations bring people together or push them apart, 43 percent of Americans said that religious groups help unify the country, and only 29 percent said that religion pushes people apart. When asked whether interactions with people of different religions are positive or negative, just 7 percent of the sample said that engaging with people from different faiths was a negative experience, while nearly six in ten said it was somewhat (14 percent) or mostly (44 percent) positive.

Again and again, the data points to the fact that most religious people are proponents of religious diversity. They generally believe that religious organizations have a unifying impact in their local communities and report that their interactions with people from a variety of faith backgrounds are edifying. While the voices on social media that get magnified the most are those that emphasize the differences between religious groups, the average American looks for common ground. They respect the faith of their neighbor, even when they don't believe in the same things.

Thus, a troubling disconnect emerges between what we see here and the data that was presented in the chapters that describe the trajectory of major religious groups like evangelicals, Catholics, atheists, and agnostics. White evangelicals and Catholics have swung significantly toward the right over the last several decades. Members of the clergy in those denominations have staked out increasingly conservative positions. The nonreligious are moving in the opposite direction, perceiving the Democratic Party as becoming more moderate over time, while atheists and agnostics are moving toward the leftward pole of the ideological spectrum. Yet the data in this chapter points to a much different conclusion: The average American tends to be fairly moderate, nuanced, and pragmatic in how they view some of the most talked about and divisive issues in modern society. Said succinctly, the individual-level data doesn't seem to match what is happening at the institutional level of American society.

Is There Really a Culture War?

In 1992, the Republican Party had a rising star on its hands. By any metric, Pat Buchanan was a GOP firebrand. He was deeply critical of President George H. W. Bush. He believed that the commander in chief was too willing to compromise and unwilling to stand for true conservatism. Even though doing so was verboten in partisan politics, Buchanan ran against Bush in the 1992 Republican primaries. While he didn't win any states, he managed to tally enough votes that the GOP establishment had to take the threat seriously. To appease Buchanan, the party gave him a prime-time speaking slot at the Republican National Convention. The speech was a barn burner that has lived on in political discourse for decades. He stated, "There is a religious war going on in this country. It is a cultural war, as critical to the kind of nation we shall be as the Cold War itself, for this war is for the soul of America."[5] Thus, the term "cultural war" has become a handy verbal shortcut for explaining the divisions that seem to be evident in the United States. When political commentators talk about same-sex marriage or abortion, they lump it into a large conflict about things like values and religious beliefs.

But as previously mentioned at the beginning of this chapter, political scientists aren't that certain the culture war actually exists.

One of the books that I read and reread during my studies was *Culture War? The Myth of a Polarized America*. In the introduction, the authors quote a number of political pundits and journalists who try to use culture war framing. The authors write, "The sentiments expressed . . . [by] scholars, journalists, and politicos range from simple exaggeration to sheer nonsense."[6] In his book *America's Crisis of Values: Reality and Perception*, Wayne Baker states plainly, "The culture war is largely a fiction."[7] In 2013, political scientist William Jacoby found that while there may be some significant cleavages in American society based on partisanship, "the empirical evidence does not signal the presence of a culture war that emanates from a religious divide between fundamentalists and the rest of the American population."[8]

Still, anyone reading this book would likely say that the United States *feels* divided. Scholars working in this area have come to the consensus that while polarization at the rank-and-file level is probably overstated, there is strong evidence of what has been described as "affective polarization." This is the idea that individuals are generating stronger negative emotions toward political opponents and increased feelings of warmth for those whom they view as "on their side." In other words, the culture war is more about "us versus them" than about policy positions on hot-button issues. As the data in this chapter makes clear, the average American is not on either extreme edge of the abortion debate. Additionally, the typical Christian (and even the average evangelical) is not entirely convinced of some of the most basic Christian doctrines, such as belief in Jesus being the only pathway to salvation. Most Christian parents would not be unhappy if their son or daughter married someone from a different faith background.

What seems to be happening is that the average American is becoming more and more convinced that they should at least feign support for the most strident voices in their tribe. For Christians, this is often the preachers who spend their days trying to stoke the fires of affective polarization. These are people who make a living by ridiculing mainline Protestants for not being Christian enough or Muslims, Buddhists, and atheists for not being Christian at all. On the other side, the loudest voices in modern atheism have made progressive politics their orthodoxy. While one is encouraged to explore either atheist or agnostic perspectives, considering whether there might be only two genders is the kind of inquiry that will get one ostracized.

The data points to the simple fact that there are a whole lot of people on both sides of the religious divide who listen to the thought leaders of their respective tribes and just can't believe everything they are hearing. However, they do agree that the other side is clearly wrong and deserves to be ridiculed for belonging to a different tribe. That's the real tragedy of the current discourse. Questioning the prevailing opinions of one's own group once or twice is acceptable, but like-minded people quickly tire of such inquiries. So, for an individual who feels out of sync with their chosen social group, only two options are available: They can go through the difficult process of switching sides, or they can simply keep their doubts, worries, and questions to themselves. The data seems to suggest that many people take this second route, simply because it's easier.

A couple years ago, I was part of a research team that fielded a survey among evangelicals that asked about women in leadership, something that groups like the Southern Baptist Convention had strongly opposed. We stated, "Assuming the women in question have the appropriate training and certification, would you agree or disagree that they can lead in the following roles." Then respondents were given four scenarios ranging from teaching a Sunday school class to preaching from behind the pulpit on Sunday morning. In this sample, 87 percent of evangelicals had no issue with a female Sunday school teacher, and just 27 percent of them said that they would not want a woman to preach a Sunday sermon. Of course, this data was met with a tremendous amount of backlash by Southern Baptist leaders.

One prominent theologian who has a daily podcast just could not believe these results to be true. He questioned the validity of the research methods and the construction of the survey questions, but he also made a pretty simple argument: If the majority of Southern Baptists truly believe that women should hold the title of pastor, why don't hundreds of SBC churches have women in the pulpit each Sunday? My answer is simple: Many rank-and-file Southern Baptists would prefer that women have full access to leadership, but they realize that it's easier to sit on their hands and not speak up. They just don't find the issue important enough to allow it to ruin the good friendships they have formed in their local churches. Go along to get along. And the upshot is that even though a whole lot of people are more moderate than their religious tradition, not enough are willing to speak up about that fact.

10

Not All Is Lost

THE BIG TAKEAWAYS

- There are lots of reasons to worry about the future of American religion and American democracy.
- There are practical ways that people can resist being sorted into one side or the other of the political debate.

In 2022, the culture warriors managed to find a new point of conflict. For decades, it had centered on the institution of marriage and whether two people of the same gender could enter into the same union as heterosexual couples. In *Obergefell v. Hodges*, the Supreme Court ruled that the fundamental right to marry extended to same-sex couples. As soon as that ruling came down, making same-sex marriage the law of the land, the cultural warriors had to find new battleground. It took a few years, but eventually a consensus began to emerge.

In small towns and big cities alike, school board meetings turned into shouting matches as concerned parents voiced their displeasure about their tax dollars being used to buy books that centered LGBTQ+ characters. Librarians were called on the carpet to explain their purchasing decisions, and many of them faced threats of violence because of the books they made available to children in their buildings.

One especially prescient moment took place at a school board meeting held in Dearborn, Michigan, in October 2022. Dearborn is often considered to be the epicenter of Islam in the United States and has the largest mosque in the country. Politically, Dearborn is left of center. Joe Biden won 74 percent of the Dearborn votes that were cast in 2020. However, in the Democratic primary, the most liberal candidate on the ballot, Bernie Sanders, defeated Biden by thirty percentage points. In other words, Dearborn is not a haven of MAGA Americans.

Even so, hundreds of Muslim Americans gathered at the school board meeting to express their displeasure over materials that seemed to promote LGBTQ+ identity and inclusion. While one parent who spoke to *The Guardian* stated, "This has nothing to do with Trump,"[1] there was a clear sense from that gathering that a new political coalition might be forming among Muslims and white evangelicals. While Muslims and evangelicals vehemently disagree on theology, they could find common cause on this specific issue.

An ancient proverb says, "The enemy of my enemy is my friend." In this case, it seems as though evangelicals and Muslims have realized that while they may have very little in common in other aspects of their lives, they can set that aside to work for the same political outcome.

In my estimation, this is what the future of American religion and politics looks like. As the share of Americans who are religious continues to decline, there will be two ramifications of such a profound demographic shift. The first is that the religious people who remain will be more committed to their faith than ever. Consider a metaphor from the culinary world. One of the most basic skills is how to make a reduction sauce. The cook puts a large amount of liquid into a pot on the stove. They add herbs and spices and bring it to a simmer. If one were to taste the broth at this stage, it would have very little flavor. However, over time, the heat begins to turn some of the liquid in the pot into steam, which evaporates. After a few hours and some occasional stirring, there's a lot less liquid in the pot, and the chef is left with a thick concoction whose flavors are incredibly concentrated.

The people who are left in America's great religions are like this leftover concentration of potent flavors. They are the true believers. They agree with the church's dogma, they are fully enmeshed in the culture of their religion, and they are present every time the church's doors are open. In other words, they may be smaller in number, but their voices are louder in the public square. To use a political science term, they are ideologues. They are the ones who will knock on doors for their preferred candidate, they will work hours at phone banks to get out the vote, and they will cast a ballot in even the most inconsequential primary election.

Remaining Believers Are More Strident

One of the most common questions I get is this: "Are younger Christians more moderate than their parents and grandparents?" For instance, there's a well-organized group called Young Evangelicals for Climate Action that is often covered by media outlets. When people read about this group, they are convinced that the next generation of teens and young adults is going to change the narrative surrounding the political views of evangelical Christians. Or they will hear a story about a church buying up medical debt for pennies on the dollar and then forgiving those obligations for people living in the community, and they will think it's part of a wider move of Christians focusing on economic equality. But what I have found over and over is that younger Christians are just as conservative as the people who are forty or fifty years older sitting beside them on Sunday mornings.

In fall 2024, I managed to persuade some colleagues at the University of Illinois Springfield to include a single question on a poll that they were about to put into the field. If someone identified as an evangelical Protestant, they were asked which of these two scenarios they would rather see:

1. Twenty-five percent of Americans are devout evangelicals. Twenty-five percent are monthly attending mainline Protestants. Fifty percent are nonreligious.
2. Twenty-five percent of Americans are devout evangelicals. Seventy-five percent are nonreligious.

The impetus behind the question was straightforward. I wanted to understand how much animus evangelicals had toward mainline Protestants. In other words, would they rather see a nation where people were either clearly devout or clearly nonreligious, or would they prefer one with people from a wider swath of the religious landscape, even if some weren't so committed to the faith? The top line result comports largely with the data that I discussed in chapter 9. In the entire sample of evangelicals, just 14 percent of them preferred a world that was 25 percent evangelicals and 75 percent nonreligious Americans. The conclusion from this survey question is simple: Very few evangelicals wanted to see the mainline disappear and be replaced by more nones.

When I poked and prodded the data on various metrics, not many differences emerged on this question. For instance, the responses of male and female evangelicals were statistically the same. In terms of education, an evangelical with a high school diploma had exactly the same view as an evangelical who had a graduate degree. Even church attendance didn't matter that much. Among evangelicals who attended yearly, 17 percent preferred a world with 75 percent nones; the number was 11 percent among evangelicals who attended church every week. There was, however, one specific demographic variable that produced a significant difference: age (see fig. 10.1).

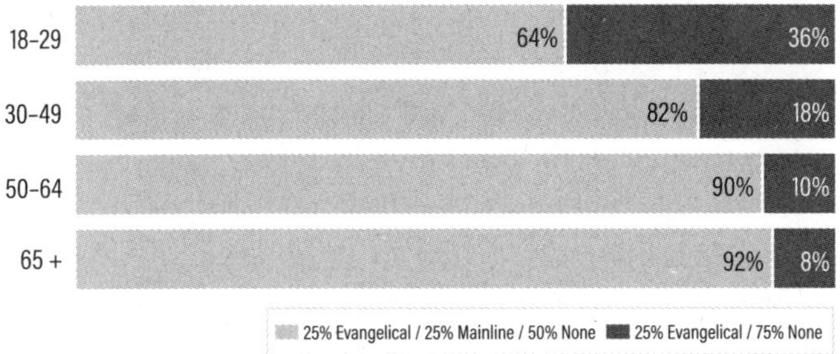

Figure 10.1 The preferred religious future for the United States among evangelicals by age, 2024

Among self-identified evangelicals who were at least fifty years old, almost none of them preferred a world that was 25 percent evangelicals and 75 percent nonreligious. In fact, over 90 percent of them indicated that they would rather see more mainline Protestants and fewer nones. However, among the youngest evangelicals in the sample, those ages eighteen to twenty-nine, 36 percent of them said that they preferred a world with no marginally active mainline Protestants. Remember, in the entire sample, just 14 percent of evangelicals took this position. Young evangelicals were 2.5 times more likely to prefer a world that was 25 percent evangelicals and 75 percent nones.

Why are younger evangelicals much more polarized in their thinking than older evangelicals? Because, to return to our cooking metaphor, they are the viscous liquid remaining in the stockpot after the reduction. Many young people who grew up in evangelical churches left during high school or during their early college years. They couldn't agree with the doctrines, the politics, or the culture of American evangelicalism. That left fewer and fewer of them in the youth groups on Wednesday nights. Which means that the social pressure to leave the church was greater for them than any prior generation.

Imagine being an evangelical high school student who sits in class next to someone who identifies as bisexual and another who is going through a gender transition. Having to defend a worldview that is increasingly in the minority in your immediate environment can lead to only two possible outcomes. One is to leave the faith behind entirely, while the other is to dig in your heels and become more steadfast in your resolve to defend your religion to your peers.

Older evangelicals grew up in an environment that was much more amenable to religion. Even into the 1970s, about 90 percent of all American adults said that they were Christian. It was unusual in those days to find someone who said that they were atheist and probably even rarer to encounter an individual who wanted to question basic Christian doctrine. Thus, there was no strong sense of the Religious Right versus the secular left, because it wasn't numerically a fair fight. The result was a faith that went largely unchallenged and a type of cultural religiosity that valued things like diversity of beliefs and respect for other Christian traditions.

Another development as religious people become a smaller minority in the United States is that those who embrace Christianity are coming to understand that it is not a viable strategy for the future to stir up animosities between Protestants and Catholics or between Christians and Muslims. As the story from Dearborn illustrates, while evangelicals and Muslims disagree on nearly every core religious doctrine, they are united in their belief that some books should be banned from the school library. In the 2020 presidential election, Muslims were the religious group most likely to vote for Joe Biden—who garnered 93 percent of their votes. Meanwhile, 81 percent of white evangelicals voted for Donald Trump. These groups could not be more divided at the ballot box. But during that school board meeting, they spoke with nearly the same voice.

We often forget that there has been a tremendous amount of religious conflict in the United States even among groups that share a common Christian heritage. Famous evangelist Billy Graham was strongly opposed to the candidacy of John F. Kennedy based on his Catholic affiliation. He went so far as to conduct a secret meeting in Switzerland in August 1960 to which he invited twenty-five American church leaders, including famed preacher Norman Vincent Peale. Peale's wife wrote to a friend during that convening, saying, "[The attendees] were unanimous in feeling that the Protestants in America must be aroused in some way, or the solid block Catholic voting, plus money, will take this election."[2] A few weeks later, Peale remarked of the upcoming election, "Our American culture is at stake. I don't say it won't survive, but it won't be what it was."[3]

Yet in 1994, a group of prominent evangelicals, including Charles Colson and Pat Robertson, locked arms with Catholic leaders, including Cardinal John O'Connor, to sign a statement called "Evangelicals & Catholics Together: The Christian Mission in the Third Millennium." Its purpose was to publicly declare that both traditions were in harmony on many key doctrines. Disheartened by a growing tension between the two faiths in places like Eastern Europe and Latin America, the signatories made clear that what held Catholics and evangelicals together was much stronger than what divided them. But they were also forceful in noting that it was more important than ever for Christians to unite to oppose what they saw as the biggest threat. "In our so-called developed societies, a widespread secularization increasingly descends into a moral, intellectual, and spiritual nihilism that denies not only the One who is the Truth but the very idea of truth itself."[4] While they could have differences of opinion on the pope and on what happens to the elements during Communion, they could all agree that the rise of the nones was the real enemy.

Thus, the future of American religion and politics could best be described as strange bedfellows. All the anti-Catholic animosity that was a key feature of American Christianity for hundreds of years has largely dissipated. In the immediate aftermath of the September 11, 2001, attacks, several prominent evangelical leaders took aim at Islam. For instance, in November 2001, Franklin Graham called Islam "a very evil and wicked religion,"[5] and less than a year later, Jerry Vines, then pastor of First Baptist Church of Jacksonville,

Florida, and previously president of the Southern Baptist Convention, called the prophet Muhammad a "demon-possessed pedophile."[6] In 2014, the Pew Research Center asked respondents to place a variety of religious groups on a scale from 0 (meaning they felt very cold toward them) to 100 (meaning they felt very warm toward them). Among white evangelicals, Muslims' average score was just 30. The only group they felt cooler toward was atheists.[7] In a poll I conducted with Tony Jones in 2024, the average thermometer score for Muslims among white evangelicals was 50. That's fairly compelling evidence that the typical evangelical has moved from a position of animosity to a position of ambivalence toward followers of Islam in just a decade. In addition, while Catholics and evangelicals don't agree on everything, they are becoming increasingly aware that they are part of a shrinking minority and that locking arms is the most effective way to push back against the nones.

As people of faith shrink in numbers but also become more militant, certain, and unified in their positions, the resulting religious environment is at odds with the overarching religious sentiment in the United States fifty or seventy-five years ago. In December 1952, President Dwight Eisenhower, speaking about the philosophical principles that founded the United States, stated, "Our form of government has no sense unless it is founded in a deeply felt religious faith, and I don't care what it is. Of course, it is the Judeo-Christian concept, but it must be a religion with all men being created equal."[8] Think about how much that statement stands at odds with a current strain of Christian nationalism that argues that the United States is an explicitly Christian nation and that Christians deserve special treatment and privileges over people from other religious traditions.

Still a Religious Country

The growing religious, social, and cultural chasm between this remnant of religious people and the increasing number of zealous

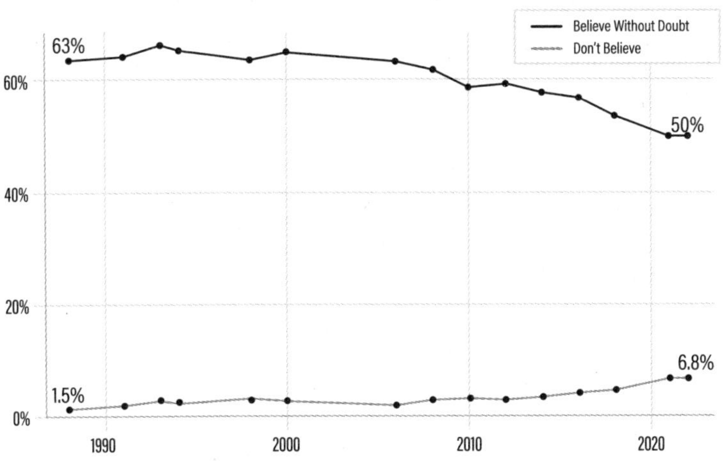

Figure 10.2 Belief in God among American adults, 1988–2022

nonreligious Americans is where a huge number of Americans find themselves, feeling like they don't fit neatly into either camp. If we look at the data, what we find over and over is that, although the numbers of those who indicate they have no religious affiliation have risen from about 5 percent of the United States in 1991 to nearly 30 percent in the most recent data, a lot of people still have a strong sense of religious conviction. The General Social Survey has been asking people about God's existence since 1988. They are given a series of six statements ranging from "I don't believe in God" to "I know God really exists and I have no doubts about it." When we trace the survey's statistics over the last thirty-five years, a fairly steady pattern emerges (see fig. 10.2).

In 1988, it was nearly impossible to find anyone who said that they did not believe in God at all. In the entire sample of 1,481 respondents, just 22 of them—less than 2 percent—took an atheist view. At the same time, the share of folks who chose the most certain "I have no doubts" option was a strong majority (63 percent). Through the next several decades, it's surprising just how little changed on these measures given how much scholars talk about the rapidly increasing secularism of the United States. Even in 2022, half the sample indicated that they had some faith in God. That's a decline of just thirteen percentage points over a period of thirty-four years. At the same time, the proportion of people who hold the position that God doesn't exist was still incredibly low—less than 7 percent. In 2022, for every person who said there was no God, there were seven Americans who believed in God without a doubt.

It's also clear from Cooperative Election Study data that the average American still believes that religion plays an important role in their lives (see fig. 10.3). The survey asks, "How important is religion in your life?" with responses ranging from "very important" to "not at all important." In 2008, the most popular choice among those taking the survey was "very important"—selected by nearly half of respondents. Both the "not too important" and the "not at all important" responses combined for just 27 percent of the sample. It's key to note that the two middle options have not changed in a statistically significant way over time. The portion

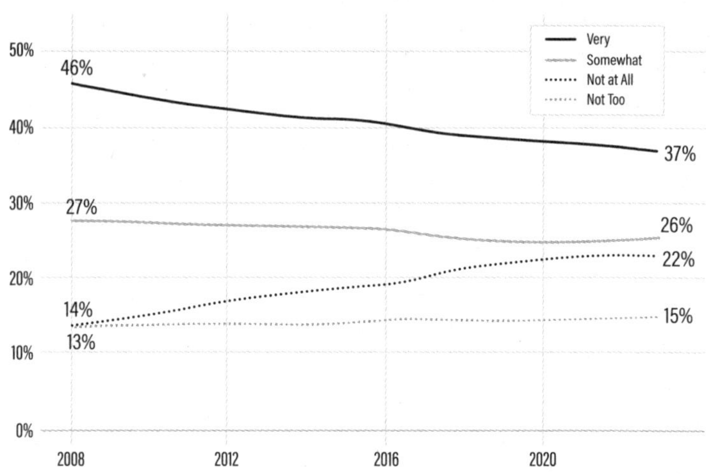

Figure 10.3 Religious importance among American adults, 2008–22

that said religion was "somewhat important" declined by a single percentage point between 2008 and 2022, while the share who said "not too important" rose by just two points. Only the edges moved. The "not at all important" share rose by eight points, while the "very important" share dropped by a corresponding nine points. But in 2022, the portion of Americans who chose one of the top two options was still nearly two in three American adults (63 percent).

The data tells a fairly compelling story that, despite all the news to the contrary, the United States remains highly religious among developed nations. In the 2022 General Social Survey, among people who reported never attending religious services, 25 percent of them still said that they believed in God with certainty, while only 17 percent of them said that God doesn't exist. While this book has made it clear that the outward signs of religiosity have declined rapidly over the last several decades, it's a mistake to say that secularism has taken over the United States. About 85 percent of Americans believe in God in some way, over 60 percent of Americans identify with a Christian tradition, and 55 percent of adults attend religious services at least once a year. Recall from chapter 9 that the share of Americans who were not nones but also didn't identify as born-again was nearly 60 percent around 1990. Today, that number is down to approximately 40 percent. That means that two in five adult Americans are feeling even more confused and isolated as religious polarization has taken hold.

Being Reasonable People

I've been a part of a lot of organizations in my life—workplaces, churches, and community groups. On several occasions, I've been asked to be part of a committee to choose a new colleague or a member to sit on a governing board. The one thing I ask in guiding my decision is, "Is this a reasonable person?" I want to be around people who are levelheaded, are willing to see both sides, and possess the social intelligence to know when to stop pushing to get more out of a negotiation and realize that both sides have compromised enough. In my mind, many people who are in the middle of the far left and far right factions of the political spectrum are reasonable people. They aren't bomb throwers, but neither are they wishy-washy. Yet what I've come to realize over the last several years is that it's harder and harder to be a reasonable person in a world where a small but very vocal contingent thinks about the world in black-and-white binaries and wants everyone else to share their worldview.

There are, however, a few guiding principles that I have picked up along the way that help me keep my bearings and stay level-headed, even when the rhetoric gets heated and emotions start to creep in. I will be the first to admit that I am not always able to stick to my highest ideals, but if my faith has taught me anything, it's simply this: We are all sinners in need of a little grace. I need to be willing to extend grace to other people, but I also should not beat myself up when I fall short of my highest ideals for behavior and decorum.

Principle Number 1: Learn to Spot Fringe Beliefs

There's a concept in political science called the "median voter theorem." It posits that the distribution of public opinion across the electorate looks like a bell curve. It's high in the middle and very low on the sides. In other words, if we aggregated the opinions of all Americans on a variety of issues from health care to immigration to abortion, a big swath of the country would be found in the middle. Thus, a Republican running for office would be well served staking out issue positions that are just to the right of center, while Democrats would be well served portraying a message that is just to the left of the midpoint. That would maximize each politician's ability to get as many votes as possible.

However, across social media, whether it be X or TikTok or Facebook, the most fringe beliefs tend to go viral. For instance, there seems to be an incredibly loud chorus of voices online seeking to make abortion completely illegal, with no exceptions for rape, incest, or the life of the woman. These people also believe that anyone who aids or participates in an abortion procedure—from the woman to the gynecologist to the receptionist who booked the appointment—should face criminal penalties. These "abortion abolitionists" post this sentiment often, and it quickly gets shared by hundreds if not thousands of other accounts. It's fairly easy to look at the number of shares and see the video views on YouTube for such a position and think, *Wow, this must be an incredibly popular way to look at this issue.*

In 2024, the Cooperative Election Study included a battery of questions about the legality of abortion in different circumstances. One of the statements was simply, "Make abortion illegal in all circumstances." Among the entire sample of sixty thousand American adults, just 11 percent agreed. If the sample is restricted to just white Protestants who self-identified as evangelicals, the share who supported a total ban on abortion was 21 percent. Even when the sample is restricted to white evangelicals who attend church at least once a week, support for a total ban was just 28 percent. The abortion abolitionist position, empirically speaking, is a fringe position among the general public, and it is a distinct minority view even among the religiously devout and politically conservative segment of the American electorate.

In 2024, my colleague Paul Djupe and I were invited to work with the Freedom from Religion Foundation (FFRF), a nonprofit organization with the stated goal of "educating the public on nontheism and promoting the constitutional principle of separation between church and state." As part of the project, we conducted a survey of the membership of the FFRF alongside a random sample survey of nonreligious Americans. Of the 11,422 members of the FFRF surveyed, just fifty-six individuals said that they planned to vote for Donald Trump in the upcoming election. On a question about political ideology, 88 percent of FFRF members said that they were liberal. That was twenty-one percentage points higher than our random sample of nonreligious Americans and fifty-four points higher than a random sample of Americans from all religious affiliations. In other words, the FFRF is about as far left as it gets. But when respondents were given this statement, "I support reparations for the descendants of enslaved people," they nearly split down the middle, with 47 percent in favor.

When less than 30 percent of weekly-attending white evangelicals agree that abortion should be criminalized, and when less than half of FFRF members agree that the federal government should provide reparations, it's fair to assume that both positions can be considered outside the political mainstream. Now, let me be clear, I have absolutely no problem with an individual speaking up passionately in favor of either position. Free speech is one of the most beautiful and empowering privileges of being an American. What I do not support is someone on the fringe of either side of a debate thinking that people in the middle are morally defective for not agreeing with them. Though logistically impossible, it would be incredibly helpful if there were little notes at the bottom of social media posts that told us what percent of Americans actually agreed with the views of the content creators. For many, that would be more than enough to stop them from engaging the debate.

The way I see it, a person who holds a fringe belief has three options in how to proceed when they are made aware of this fact. The first is to try to convince a majority of the public that their view is correct and should be adopted. I think this is the most American way to tackle this problem. The marketplace of ideas is one of the most powerful forces in the United States. A belief holder should try to convince people why prevailing views are incorrect and why this new political position should be adopted. That's how real change has been made in America.

Consider one of the most consequential cases in American legal history—*Dred Scott v. Sandford*. Dred Scott was an enslaved person in Missouri, a state that permitted slavery. His owner took him to Wisconsin, a free state. Scott sued for his freedom, and the case eventually landed in the Supreme Court, which decided it in 1857. In what is often considered its worst decision of all time, the justices ruled that Scott had no constitutional standing to sue in court because he was not a citizen of the United States. Yet less than five years later, Abraham Lincoln issued the Emancipation Proclamation, which effectively ended the institution of slavery. Several pieces of legislation in the last 150 years, like the Civil Rights Act of 1964 and the Voting Rights Act of 1965, not only rejected the views of the court in the Dred Scott decision but also took additional measures to ensure that African Americans would enjoy equal citizenship rights under the law. The anti-slavery movement changed the law by winning the hearts and minds of the average American.

Of course, another option available to a fringe belief holder is to force their opinion on the American public through the passage of unpopular legislation. That was certainly the case with the Eighteenth Amendment, which prohibited the production, sale, and transportation of alcohol for consumption. While the data indicates that alcohol consumption declined in the United States when the amendment went into effect in 1920, it proved to be almost impossible to enforce. Organized crime began to bootleg whiskey at an alarming rate, and many police officers chose either to look the other way or to take kickbacks to allow the illicit trade to expand. In 1932, Franklin Roosevelt campaigned on repealing the Eighteenth Amendment, which came to fruition with the passage of the Twenty-First Amendment in 1933. While there were certainly noble aims in trying to curtail alcohol consumption, laws are effective only when the average American sees them as worthwhile. The same principle applies to the topic of abortion. The Supreme Court's decision in *Dobbs v. Jackson Women's Health Organization* left each state to decide how it would regulate the procedure. Fourteen states effectively banned abortion, yet data from the Guttmacher Institute indicates that abortions rose 11 percent between 2020 and 2023.[9] There are dozens of examples in American history of the public simply ignoring laws that it finds unpalatable. In terms of long-term success, it's hard to argue that the Eighteenth Amendment or the *Dobbs* ruling had the impact that supporters desired.

There is one other option, however, that is always on the table for a fringe belief holder: Burn it all down. A few years ago, Danish political scientist Michael Bang Petersen became interested in understanding why fringe beliefs tend to spread like wildfire on the internet.[10] He began to notice a pattern among people who share conspiracy theories: One day they will amplify stories that make Democrats look bad, and the next day they will share information that can be damaging to Republicans. He began to form a theory that a small but vocal number of Americans could be described by a quote from the movie *The Dark Knight*: "Some men just want to watch the world burn." So he started including statements on surveys like, "We cannot fix the problems in our social institutions; we need to tear them down and start over."

What Petersen found was that about 5 percent of voters could be described as having a "need for chaos." They felt so aggrieved and hopeless that the only solution that they thought made any sense was to dismantle the systems of government and economics and hope something better emerged from the rubble. This should go without saying, but as someone who read the literature about democratization, I think it's highly unlikely that what would emerge out of the ashes of the American empire would be better than what we have now. But for those who hold fringe beliefs, this may be seen as the only possible avenue for them to see their political views materialize into actual change.

Of course, I think most readers of this book will quickly realize that the second and third options—push unpopular legislation or burn it all to the ground—are not viable pathways forward in a thriving, pluralistic democracy. I have studied political science my entire adult life, and one thing that I know is that the best way to make change in a society like the United States is from the ground up. Persuading people through any reasonable means is the only surefire way to bring about significant and durable change.

Consider the fact that evangelical and Catholic leaders have been exhorting their followers for fifty years about the horrors of abortion. They make the theological claim that when a sperm meets an egg, a human being is conceived. However, the share of Americans who identified as pro-choice was at the same level in 2022 as in 1995.[11] While the Southern Baptist Convention passed a resolution against in vitro fertilization at its annual meeting in the summer of 2024, data from the Pew Research Center indicated that only 8 percent of white evangelicals viewed IVF as a bad thing that same year.[12] Why have religious leaders been so ineffective at convincing even their own flocks that their theological positions are the moral, just, and right ones? This question should lead to some real soul-searching among people of faith.

Principle Number 2: The Perfect Is the Enemy of the Good

In 2023, *The Washington Post*'s Perry Bacon Jr. wrote an essay about his religious background for his regular column. Bacon had been raised in the Black church tradition, where his father was an assistant pastor for a small congregation in Louisville, Kentucky. Bacon wrote about how his congregation took up a collection before he went to college and presented him with a few hundred dollars to help him pay for books and tuition. In his twenties and thirties, Bacon bounced around the world of nondenominational Protestantism, remaining active but doubting some of the core tenets of Christianity. Then he began fading away from his church. The cause wasn't one specific thing, just a growing discontent with various aspects of Christianity (including its link to Republican politics). The pandemic gave Bacon an easy excuse not to attend at all.

For Bacon, what makes it even more difficult to return is that he now has a young, inquisitive daughter. He writes, "I don't want to take her to a place that has a specific view of the world as well as answers to the big questions and then have to explain to Charlotte that some people agree with all of the church's ideas, Dad agrees with only some and many other people don't agree with any."[13] Bacon fully recognizes the many social and ethical benefits of being part of a church, but he just can't get himself (or his daughter) to make it back to a house of worship. It's a refrain that I hear when I talk to people about why they left the church: They got tired of gritting their teeth and shaking their heads during parts of the sermon or Bible study. Bacon's op-ed was widely praised by readers for its honesty, receiving nearly six thousand comments on the newspaper's website.

A few days after Bacon's essay was published, Ross Douthat, a *New York Times* columnist, wrote a thoughtful response entitled "Where Should Agnostics Go on Sundays?" His main argument is that we all should become comfortable with the idea that we may experience some discomfort attending church regularly. Douthat believes that being confronted with ideas that we disagree with should not be a reason to avoid going to Sunday worship; it should be the thing that draws us to attend. Douthat writes, "Obviously, you don't want to lay too much ambiguity on a three-year-old. But if you're going to raise your kids with some metaphysical ambiguity, no matter what, then 'We go to a church that believes X because we think church has a lot to offer you, even though Dad only believes in some of X' seems like an entirely honest thing to tell children."[14] In other words, parents can use those instances as teachable moments regarding the value of being exposed to ideas that we sometimes disagree with.

For reasons that are hard to articulate and even harder to measure, it seems like a growing number of Americans have become obsessed with the idea of authenticity. For years, it was a buzzword in some Christian circles: "We want to create an authentic community of Christ followers." People often use that word in nonreligious contexts too. They conceptualize the goal of their lives as "being authentic" to their "true selves." One consequence is that people say they can't work for a company unless they align completely with its operating principles. Or they can't date someone who doesn't align with them on a whole list of core values. It seems like it's become a virtue to not compromise on these types of things.

The upshot of this endless quest for authenticity is that lots of people feel like they can't join a church because either they don't fully believe in all the core theology of the congregation or they disagree with the church's policy on issues related to gender or sexual orientation. In other words, unless they can find a local congregation that checks every single box of their core values, joining would be inauthentic. The assumption that nonchurchgoers seem to have is that all committed church members completely agree with the leadership and theology of their houses of worship.

The pursuit of the ideal church is an exercise in futility. I think for some it serves as an excuse to not become involved in a local church community. Others just don't want to feel uncomfortable when the pastor talks about gender roles or a biblical sexual ethic.

When I was working on my dissertation, I agonized over every punctuation mark and each citation. I wanted to make sure that the correct words were italicized and that everything was formatted just the right way. Fidgeting with all these details became somewhat of an obsession for me. As progress on my dissertation stalled, one of the professors on my committee pulled me into his office and told me something life-changing: "The perfect is the enemy of the good." It's a saying that has been traced back to Voltaire but appears in numerous forms in literary history, and it speaks to a problem that we often face. We want everything to be "just so," and in pursuit of that we miss out on something that is much better. In my case, I was missing out on the joy of earning my doctoral degree because I was more interested in finding every typographical error.

The right style of music, the appropriate amount of Scripture reading, or the ideal sermon length is certainly worth considering when selecting a new spiritual home. As is the church's view of the Bible, the role women play in congregational leadership, and who is eligible to receive Communion. But if you are looking for a church that checks every single box on your church wish list, you will always be searching. And as I've made clear in the previous chapters, you shouldn't seek out a church where everyone votes for the same candidates and shares a similar worldview. Agreeing with the sermon most of the time is a reasonable expectation for a place to put down roots.

Exposing ourselves to differences from both the pulpit and the pews is essential for the future of American religion and American democracy. It's also good for one's own well-being. Finding points of agreement while also being willing to talk through areas of difference allows us to strengthen our intellectual muscle. It expands our worldview and extends our empathy for those who are different from us. On these measures, many congregations more than fit the bill. Stop seeking the perfect church for you and just pick one that's "good enough." Your presence there will make it better.

Principle Number 3: Don't Dehumanize the Other

With all the data analysis included in this book, I hope one thing becomes apparent: Religious spaces are more homogeneous today than at any point in the last fifty years. White Christianity is increasingly becoming politically homogeneous—with Republicans outnumbering Democrats four to one. But religious spaces are also losing diversity in a number of other dimensions as well—education level, social class, and family composition. In a healthy and thriving democratic society, houses of worship need to be places where people from all backgrounds and political persuasions can sit side by side in pews and say the Lord's Prayer together. There's something simple yet profound about mingling with people who are different—the social literature is unequivocal about the value of being in diverse social spaces.

In 1954, social psychologist Gordon Allport published *The Nature of Prejudice*, an incredibly important book that's still assigned in colleges and universities. The historical backdrop of Allport's work was a concerted effort by policy experts and academics to explore ways to further integrate housing projects that were sprouting up all over America due to rapid population expansion during the baby boom. Allport went in search of a way to help different racial groups feel comfortable living in close quarters with one another. His contribution to the field is simply called "contact theory," and it has a straightforward premise: Intergroup contact under appropriate conditions can reduce prejudice between majority and minority group members. Basically, hanging out with people from a different background usually results in greater trust and less animus.

However, there's a key component in Allport's description that is worth reflecting on: "under appropriate conditions." Dropping a dozen random people on a desert island with no food and little water and asking them to survive for two weeks is not an environment conducive to reducing prejudice among individuals. Instead, Allport says that four criteria are necessary for contact theory to flourish:

1. Equal status among group members
2. Common goals that highlight interdependence
3. A focus on cooperation, not competition
4. Support of authorities, laws, and customs[15]

There is one social space that seems to check most of these boxes: houses of worship. While most churches tend to have some kind of leadership structure, the majority of people are on equal footing in the congregation. Many religious congregations work on common goals like serving the community, and the only way to accomplish that is to work together. I've been around churches enough to know that very few people head up a ministry or chair a committee to receive some kind of public recognition. They just want to see the work being done. Also, my experience in and around churches is that local governments, law enforcement, and average people in the community are not looking to get in the way of churches doing good works—just the opposite, in fact. Basically, there's no better place for contact theory to thrive than the local church. Yet, that is not happening because houses of worship have become so socially and politically homogeneous.

When we aren't around people who are different from us, it becomes so easy to demonize and mischaracterize them. It's easy to cast aspersions on someone who votes for a candidate from the political party we don't like when we don't personally know anyone whose politics differs much from ours. It's a different story when we encounter them regularly. Imagine that you've been in Sunday school for years with a guy named Bob. You've chatted with him about family and sports. He came over once and helped you move a piece of heavy furniture into your house. Then one day he mentions in passing that he is going to support a candidate for governor that you loathe. Would you immediately end your relationship with Bob? I don't think you would. Instead, you would probably think, *I know Bob and I like Bob. He loves his family, he loves his church, he tries to be a good person and live out his faith as best he can. I just happen to disagree with his politics*. The simple act of not cutting him out of your life is the direct result of Allport's contact theory.

Unfortunately, when we don't know anyone like Bob, things quickly go awry. In the early 1990s, there was a brewing tension between two of the largest tribes in the country of Rwanda—the Hutus and the Tutsis. The result of that tension was one of the worst genocides since the Holocaust. Over a span of one hundred days in 1994, Hutu militias killed at least half a million Tutsis and likely sexually assaulted between 250,000 and 500,000. In May of that year, *Time* ran a cover with the following quote: "'There are no devils left in Hell,' the missionary said. 'They are all in Rwanda.'"[16] In the years after the tragedy, scholars have examined the event in detail and learned a number of important lessons about how such atrocities occur. In 2011, William Donohue published a paper analyzing radio broadcasts in Rwanda in the months leading up to the genocide. He found that the speakers used dehumanizing language to describe the other side—calling them "vermin" and "rats," not human beings.[17] This rhetoric gave hearers tacit permission to remove the pestilence. Because they weren't people, they were an infestation.

While I do not believe that the United States is headed toward political or civil war, I am becoming increasingly alarmed with the rhetoric used in American discourse. Often we hear conservative Christians call people who vote for Democrats "baby killers." Meanwhile, Democrats often call supporters of Donald Trump "fascists" or "racists." Remember the story of Bob from Sunday school? Imagine calling your friend, who had helped you out on a regular basis over a period of years, a name like that. Of course you wouldn't, because you know Bob and you have examined his character. We can't reduce the complexities of a vote on Election Day to a dehumanizing epithet. That kind of language doesn't invite conversations; it stops any chance we may have of a productive dialogue.

There's a theological concept that can be found in the very first chapter of the Bible: "So God created mankind in his own image, in the image of God he created them" (Gen. 1:27). Simply put, every human being is born in the image and likeness of God. It's such a simple idea but should have profound implications for anyone who calls themselves a person of faith. It means that when a person puts on a hood and joins a march for the Ku Klux Klan, they are still made in God's likeness. The same can be said for someone who wears a bandanna and a hoodie and joins a protest for the cause of antifa. They are image bearers of God. It means that God's care for the unborn equals his concern for the person who entered the United States illegally from Central America. The *imago Dei* calls us to see the dignity and worth of the people who cast ballots for Democrats or Republicans on Election Day. We can have vast disagreements about the future of the country and the role of faith in creating a "more perfect union," but we cannot compromise on seeing every person on the planet as an image bearer of the divine. Any politician who uses words or stories that dehumanize an individual or a group of people should be loudly rejected by people of faith, even if that rhetoric drives home a point that they support.

The United States: Resilient But Not Invincible

At this moment, I have never been more hopeful and more afraid for the future of the United States. No country is perfect, but I believe that the United States has brought about much more prosperity than suffering. Our democracy provided the blueprint for dozens of countries to throw off their dictators, embrace free trade, and protect human rights. Those advancements have lifted hundreds of millions of people out of abject poverty and given them a real chance at living healthy and productive lives of meaning and purpose. But I am deeply concerned that we are heading down a path of tribalism, division, and strife that imperils the future of the American experiment. I am convinced that the biggest threat facing the United States is not a foreign adversary like Russia or China. If the United States falls, it will be due to infighting, not external attacks.

I look back at the entire sweep of American history and think about all that we have overcome. We cast off the British Empire with an underfunded and poorly trained military. Then we spent decades trying to overcome the scourge of slavery—a conflict that ended in a war that set brother against brother and father against son and spilled the blood of hundreds of thousands of Americans. Then we navigated our way through the Great Depression, helped to destroy the Nazi regime, and built the United States into an unrivaled economic powerhouse. Brave men and women fought the police officers, the fire hoses, and the dogs for the possibility that people could be seen as equal under the law regardless of their skin color. Then we pulled together after a group of hijackers flew planes into the most visible symbols of American excellence. The United States is an unbelievably resilient country.

If we can survive the Revolutionary War, the War of 1812, the Civil War, the Great Depression, two world wars, the civil rights movement, and 9/11 but we are taken down by political and religious polarization, then we may not be as good as we once were. One reason I feel the need to go to church regularly is that I need to be constantly reminded of the fact that I am not as good as I think I am. May this book be a testament to the simple fact that while we have come a long way, there is much further that we need to go.

While I am under no illusion that American religion is the greatest panacea for all that ails the United States, I am convinced that the American church can be part of the solution. People gathering under one roof to sing together, pray together, and work in common cause to create a better community and a better society will certainly move us closer to the ideals that were set forth by the Founding Fathers of our country. There's nothing simpler and more consequential than people getting up on a Sunday morning, getting dressed, and making their way to a local house of worship. The fate and future of American democracy may be at stake.

Epilogue

When I began writing this book, I was pastoring a little American Baptist church in rural Illinois. I was counting attendance, hoping that we would break into the double digits. The first time we had only nine saints in the pews on a Sunday morning, it was a shock. But it quickly became commonplace. When you are down to about fifteen faithful members, losing just one person is a heavy blow.

In the first month of 2024, we experienced a number of setbacks: Our pianist had surgery, I came down with a prolonged case of strep throat, and the weather was bitterly cold. We didn't meet for four Sundays in a row. When we reconvened in early February, something felt different. Any momentum or enthusiasm that we had from prior years seemed to have evaporated. Each Sunday became more of a chore and less of a joy. The writing was on the wall.

Some conversations began to take place as the weather started to warm and we moved through the season of Lent. We needed to hold a business meeting at some point and make some clear decisions about the future of First Baptist Church. We intentionally waited until we had celebrated Easter. It felt weird to discuss the death of our church while we were also proclaiming the resurrection of our Savior. So, on the first Sunday of April, we all stuck around after I had muddled through a sermon, offered an invitation, and provided a benediction to the ten people in the pews. We held a short business meeting. It lasted about twenty minutes. A single motion was made: to hold our final worship service on July 21, 2024. That was the date closest to our very first service in July 1868. First Baptist Church would exist for 156 years, but no longer.

Those final few months were a whirlwind. All kinds of logistical questions had to be answered: Who would become the caretaker of our baptismal records? Who would get the last check from the church's operating fund? And does anyone actually want a pulpit or a lectern anymore? Several of the women of the church tackled those obstacles and many more that came up during the process of closing our doors. Our denominational leadership met with us to discuss the steps it would take to formally dissolve. I had to ask questions like, "Can I still officiate a wedding if someone asks?" The answer was a reassuring yes. Then we began to prepare for our final worship service. It felt like the process of a person in hospice planning how their funeral should be conducted. Our overarching feeling was that we wanted the service to be as normal as possible. We were still going to say the Lord's Prayer. We must recite the Apostles' Creed one last time. This was our last chance to sing the doxology and the Gloria Patri with those same voices. We knew everything was going to change after that moment, so this was our final opportunity to hold on to what had knitted us together for decades.

Then the day arrived. That last Sunday did have some special touches. We had dipped into our remaining funds to buy a nice flower arrangement for the sanctuary. We also had decided that catering a meal would be the best way to keep people around after the service to chat and reminisce. I honestly don't remember much about that last hour when I stood in front of a group of about fifty people. One thing I do know is that I was incredibly emotional. I just couldn't bury the feelings that had been building up for over seventeen years. When everything else in my life changed—I got two degrees, got married, bought a house, and had two children—that church was always there. I knew that when I walked out the door, life would never be the same.

I have now been on paid staff at three Baptist churches. At this moment, two of the three have closed their doors and the third is about 80 percent smaller than when I was attending services there two decades ago. It's hard to come to terms with the fact that every church that I've served will no longer exist in the very near future. I feel like one of those polar bears you see in a video for a wildlife advocacy organization. They are relatively content sitting on a large ice floe for a while, but it starts to shrink, so they jump off and swim to another one that they think is more stable. However, very quickly, that one begins to disintegrate into the ocean as well. And then the polar bear looks around and realizes that there aren't that many ice floes left and the ones that are still floating on the ocean's surface are farther away and harder to get to. Even if the bear can survive the swim, there's a good possibility that their new destination will be just as precarious as the previous one.

The past few months have been very disorienting. I look around at my community, which has largely become a political monoculture, and realize the churches are even more ideologically homogeneous. I've attended services with several different religious traditions since First Baptist closed—Catholics, Anglicans, Episcopalians, and Methodists. But none of them feel like home. I was talking to a friend a few weeks ago, and he asked me what I was looking for in a church. I began to describe a few characteristics and then stopped myself. I was basically telling him all the things that I loved about First Baptist. I want to go back to that, but I know that I can't. There's a famous saying from the great philosopher Heraclitus: "No man ever steps in the same river twice, for it's not the same river and he's not the same man."

I've been thinking a lot about the concept of nostalgia. It derives from the Greek and can roughly be translated as "a pain to return home." The great writer Maya Angelou perfectly encapsulates the thought when she writes, "The ache for home lives in all of us, the safe place where we can go and not be questioned."[1] I know there are tens of millions of Americans who are just like me. They believe deeply in the power of Jesus Christ and take hope in the possibility of the resurrection. They long to work hand in hand with people to build the kingdom of God in their communities and across the world. Each wants to find a safe place where they won't be questioned and they can just breathe a sigh of relief, knowing that they are home. I feel that same ache too. Every single Sunday morning.

After my church closed, I took two Sundays off. I had several invitations to visit various churches in the community and was grateful for the offers, but I needed time to decompress. Then I got up on that third Sunday and thought how easy it would be to just stay in bed, not get dressed, and not deal with all the social awkwardness that comes from being the new person in a church. But I also knew that I would be the biggest hypocrite on earth if I wrote an entire book about the value of being part of a faith community and then never attended religious services.

So on that Sunday morning I got in the shower, put on some decent clothes, and drove a couple blocks to a church that I had been thinking about for a while. When I walked in the door and scanned the pews, I quickly found three members of First Baptist all sitting together in a pew about halfway up the aisle. They were so glad to see me, and I was so relieved to see them. We sat together, trying to navigate a new order of worship and some unfamiliar songs. But then we found our rhythm when the bulletin instructed us to say the Lord's Prayer together. And our voices fell into perfect unison again, just as they did when we said those simple words so many times as members of First Baptist Church. It felt a little bit like home again.

Sources for Figures

Figures 2.1, 2.2. General Social Survey, 1972–2022.

Figure 2.3. American National Election Study, 1960–2020.

Figures 2.4, 2.5, 2.6. General Social Survey, 1972–2022.

Figure 2.7. General Social Survey, 1988–2022.

Figure 3.1. General Social Survey, 1972–2022.

Figure 3.2. Publicly available denominational records from seven major mainline Protestant denominations, 1987–2022.

Figures 3.3, 3.4, 3.5, 3.6, 4.1, 4.2, 4.3, 4.4, 4.5, 4.6. General Social Survey, 1972–2022.

Figure 4.7. Cooperative Election Study, 2020–23.

Figure 4.8. National Study of Catholic Priests, The Catholic Project, 2022, https://catholicproject.catholic.edu/national-study-of-catholic-priests.

Figures 4.9, 4.10. S. Cranney and M. Regnerus, Survey of American Catholic Priests, 2020, published September 29, 2022, https://www.thearda.com/data-archive?fid=ACATHPR1.

Figure 5.1. General Social Survey, 1972–2022.

Figure 5.2. Cooperative Election Study, 2008–23.

Figure 5.3. Cooperative Election Study, 2022–23.

Figures 5.4, 5.5, 5.6. General Social Survey, 1972–2022.

Figure 5.7. Cooperative Election Study, 2022–23.

Figures 5.8, 5.9. Cooperative Election Study, 2012–23.

Figure 5.10. Cooperative Election Study, 2020.

Figure 5.11. Cooperative Election Study, 2023.

Figure 6.1. Cooperative Election Study, 2008–23.

Figure 6.2. Nationscape Survey, 2019–21.

Figure 6.3. Cooperative Election Study, 2008–23.

Figure 6.4. General Social Survey, 1972–2018.

Figures 6.5, 6.6, 6.7, 6.8. Cooperative Election Study, 2020–23.

Figures 7.1, 7.2, 7.3, 7.4, 8.1. General Social Survey, 1972–2022.

Figure 8.2. General Social Survey, 1988–2022.

Figures 8.3, 8.4, 8.5. Cooperative Election Study, 2008–23.

Figures 8.6, 8.7, 8.8. Cooperative Election Study, 2020–23.

Figure 9.1. General Social Survey, 1988–2022.

Figure 9.2. Tricia C. Bruce, Bridget Ritz, Maureen Day, Kendra Hutchens, and Patricia Tevington, "How Americans Understand Abortion," McGrath Institute for Church Life, 2020, https://news.nd.edu/assets/395804/how_americans_understand_abortion_final_7_15_20.pdf.

Figure 9.3. Ligonier State of Theology, 2016–22, https://thestateoftheology.com.

Figure 9.4. Ligonier State of Theology, 2020–22, https://thestateoftheology.com.

Figure 9.5. R. P. Jones and M. B. Najle, "PRRI and *The Atlantic* 2018 Pluralism Survey," July 25, 2022, https://thearda.com/data-archive?fid=PRRIATL18.

Figure 10.1. Survey of American Adults fielded October 2024 by Alan Simmons, research director for the Center for State Policy and Leadership at the University of Illinois Springfield.

Figure 10.2. General Social Survey, 1988–2022.

Figure 10.3. Cooperative Election Study, 2008–22.

Notes

Chapter 1 No Place for Doubters

1. Jim Davis and Michael Graham, with Ryan P. Burge, *The Great Dechurching: Who's Leaving, Why Are They Going, and What Will It Take to Bring Them Back?* (Zondervan, 2023), xxii.

Chapter 2 Evangelicals

1. "In the Wake of the Great Awakening," *Christianity Today*, July 1989, https://www.christianitytoday.com/1989/07/in-wake-of-great-awakening.

2. H. L. Mencken, "In Memoriam: W. J. B.," *Baltimore Evening Sun*, July 27, 1925, reprinted in *The Vintage Mencken* (Knopf, 1955), 164, https://archive.org/details/mencken017105mbp/page/n181/mode/2up.

3. Karen Armstrong, *The Case for God* (Knopf, 2009), 274.

Chapter 3 Mainline Protestants

1. Mencken, quoted in Ron Chernow, *Titan: The Life of John D. Rockefeller, Sr.* (Random House, 1998), 231.

2. "2020 Group Detail Data by Nation, State, County and Metro," at "Maps and Data Files for 2020," US Religion Census, updated June 23, 2023, https://www.usreligioncensus.org/sites/default/files/2023-06/2020_USRC_Group_Detail.xlsx.

3. Dean M. Kelley, *Why Conservative Churches Are Growing: A Study in Sociology of Religion* (Harper & Row, 1972), 56–78.

4. Laurence R. Iannaccone, "Why Strict Churches Are Strong," *American Journal of Sociology* 99, no. 5 (March 1994): 1180–211, https://doi.org/10.1086/230409.

5. Paul A. Djupe and Christopher P. Gilbert, *The Prophetic Pulpit: Clergy, Churches, and Communities in American Politics* (Rowman & Littlefield, 2003).

6. Margaret Thatcher, quoted in Jim Prior, *A Balance of Power* (H. Hamilton, 1986), 106.

7. William Butler Yeats, "The Second Coming," available at Poetry Foundation, https://www.poetryfoundation.org/poems/43290/the-second-coming.

Chapter 4 American Catholics

1. Clifford A. Grammich, "Catholics in the U.S. Religion Census," US Religion Census, November 2022, https://www.usreligioncensus.org/sites/default/files/2023-05/RRA%20Catholic%20presentation.pdf.

2. Ryan Burge, "2024 Election Post-Mortem: Catholics," Graphs about Religion (website), April 28, 2025, https://www.graphsaboutreligion.com/p/2024-election-post-mortem-catholics.

3. Burge, "2024 Election Post-Mortem: Catholics."

4. Latin Mass Directory, https://www.latinmassdir.org.

5. Ruth Graham, "Old Latin Mass Finds New American Audience, Despite Pope's Disapproval," *New York Times*, November 15, 2022, https://www.nytimes.com/2022/11/15/us/latin-mass-revival.html.

6. Olga R. Rodriguez, "Archbishop: Pelosi Will Be Denied Communion Over Abortion," *Associated Press*, May 20, 2022, https://apnews.com/article/abortion-congress-nancy-pelosi-san-francisco-religion-cd68155b976a60fc4f6b948acb217858.

Chapter 5 The Nones

1. Glenn M. Vernon, "The Religious 'Nones': A Neglected Category," *Journal for the Scientific Study of Religion* 7 (1968): 219–29.

2. Jim Davis and Michael Graham, with Ryan P. Burge, *The Great Dechurching: Who's Leaving, Why Are They Going, and What Will It Take to Bring Them Back?* (Zondervan, 2023).

3. Michael Hout and Claude S. Fischer, "Why More Americans Have No Religious Preference: Politics and Generations," *American Sociological Review* 67, no. 2 (April 2002): 189, https://www.jstor.org/stable/3088891.

4. Michele F. Margolis, *From Politics to the Pews: How Partisanship and the Political Environment Shape Religious Identity* (University of Chicago Press, 2018).

5. Richard Dawkins (@RichardDawkins), "The way the non-binary faithful obsess about intersexes," X, February 1, 2024, 8:18 a.m., https://x.com/RichardDawkins/status/1753045097959100600.

6. "American Humanist Association Board Statement Withdrawing Honor from Richard Dawkins," American Humanist Association, April 19, 2021, https://americanhumanist.org/news/american-humanist-association-board-statement-withdrawing-honor-from-richard-dawkins.

7. John Piper (@JohnPiper), "Farewell Rob Bell," X (formerly Twitter), February 26, 2011, https://x.com/johnpiper/status/41590656421863424.

Chapter 6 The Great Reversal

1. Robert D. Putnam, *Bowling Alone: The Collapse and Revival of American Community* (Simon & Schuster, 2000), 22–23.

2. Karl Marx, *A Contribution to the Critique of Hegel's Philosophy of Right*, trans. Annette Jolin and Joseph O'Malley, ed. Joseph O'Malley (Cambridge University Press, 1970), 131.

3. US Census Bureau, "Median Household Income in the United States," Federal Reserve Bank of St. Louis, updated September 11, 2024, https://fred.stlouisfed.org/series/MEHOINUSA646N.

4. Ron Chernow, *Titan: The Life of John D. Rockefeller, Sr.* (Random House, 1998), 451.

5. Shaylyn Romney Garrett, "Perspective: Love Thy Neighbor, America," *Deseret News*, November 10, 2022, https://www.deseret.com/magazine/2022/11/10/23404376/class-system-religious-community-economic-mobility.

6. Mark Twain, *The Innocents Abroad, or The New Pilgrims' Progress* (Hartford, CT, 1869), 650.

Chapter 7 How the 1990s Paved the Way

1. McKay Coppins, "The Man Who Broke Politics," *Atlantic*, updated October 17, 2018, https://www.theatlantic.com/magazine/archive/2018/11/newt-gingrich-says-youre-welcome/570832.

2. Timothy McNulty and Brendan McNulty, "The Inside Story of How Newt Gingrich Single-Handedly Destroyed Congress," *Daily Beast*, August 11, 2019, https://www.thedailybeast.com/the-inside-story-of-how-newt-gingrich-single-handedly-destroyed-congress.

3. Robert D. Putnam and David E. Campbell, *American Grace: How Religion Divides and Unites Us* (Simon & Schuster, 2010), 576.

4. Ruth Braunstein, "The Backlash Against Rightwing Evangelicals Is Reshaping American Politics and Faith," *Guardian*, January 25, 2022, https://www.theguardian.com/commentisfree/2022/jan/25/the-backlash-against-rightwing-evangelicals-is-reshaping-american-politics-and-faith.

5. "Individuals Using the Internet (% of Population)—United States," World Bank Group, accessed June 12, 2025, https://data.worldbank.org/indicator/IT.NET.USER.ZS?locations=US.

Chapter 8 How Religion Became a Tribal Identity

1. Paul Froese and Christopher Bader, *America's Four Gods: What We Say About God And What That Says About Us* (Oxford University Press, 2010), 13–36.

2. E. C. Cassese and M. R. Holman, "Religion, Gendered Authority, and Identity in American Politics," *Politics and Religion* 10, no. 1 (2017): 31–56, https://doi.org/10.1017/S1755048316000407.

Chapter 9 How Polarized Are We, Really?

1. Ezra Klein, *Why We're Polarized* (Simon and Schuster, 2020).

2. Brian Montopoli, "Jon Stewart Rally: The Signs," *CBS News*, October 30, 2010, https://www.cbsnews.com/news/jon-stewart-rally-the-signs.

3. Tricia C. Bruce, "How Americans Understand Abortion," McGrath Institute for Church Life, University of Notre Dame, 2020, https://news.nd.edu/assets/395804/how_americans_understand_abortion_final_7_15_20.pdf.

4. Cathleen Falsani, "Transcript: Barack Obama and the God Factor Interview," *Sojourners*, February 21, 2012, https://sojo.net/articles/transcript-barack-obama-and-god-factor-interview.

5. Patrick Joseph Buchanan, "Culture War Speech: Address to the Republican National Convention," Houston, Texas, August 17, 1992, Voices of Democracy (website), https://voicesofdemocracy.umd.edu/buchanan-culture-war-speech-speech-text.

6. Morris P. Fiorina, with Samuel J. Abrams and Jeremy C. Pope, *Culture War? The Myth of a Polarized America*, 2nd ed. (Pearson Longman, 2006), 8.

7. Wayne E. Baker, *America's Crisis of Values: Reality and Perception* (Princeton University Press, 2005), 109.

8. W. G. Jacoby, "Is There a Culture War? Conflicting Value Structures in American Public Opinion," *American Political Science Review* 108, no. 4 (2014): 768–69.

Chapter 10 Not All Is Lost

1. Tom Perkins, "Conservative Muslims Join Forces with Christian Right on Michigan Book Bans," *Guardian*, October 16, 2022, https://www.theguardian.com/us-news/2022/oct/16/dearborn-michigan-book-bans.

2. Niall O'Dowd, "Billy Graham Tried to Stop JFK Becoming President Because He Was Catholic," Irish Central, July 12, 2022, https://www.irishcentral.com/roots/history/billy-graham-jfk-catholic.

3. "Protestant Clergy vs. the Catholic Candidate, JFK," *Time*, September 19, 1960, https://time.com/archive/6622765/protestant-clergy-vs-the-catholic-candidate-jfk.

4. Catholic-Evangelical Consultation, "Evangelicals & Catholics Together: The Christian Mission in the Third Millennium," EWTN, 1994, https://www.ewtn.com/catholicism/library/evangelicals—catholics-together-the-christian-mission-in-the-third-millennium-10976, taken from the May 1994 issue of *First Things*.

5. Council on American-Islamic Relations, "Frank Graham Claims Islam Is 'a Very Evil and Wicked Religion,'" press release, CAIR, November 19, 2001, https://www.cair.com/press_releases/frank-graham-claims-islam-is-a-very-evil-and-wicked-religion.

6. Susan Sachs, "Baptist Pastor Attacks Islam, Inciting Cries of Intolerance," *New York Times*, June 15, 2002, https://www.nytimes.com/2002/06/15/us/baptist-pastor-attacks-islam-inciting-cries-of-intolerance.html.

7. "How Americans Feel About Religious Groups," Pew Research Center, July 16, 2014, https://www.pewresearch.org/religion/2014/07/16/how-americans-feel-about-religious-groups.

8. Patrick Henry, "'And I Don't Care What It Is': The Tradition-History of a Civil Religion Proof-Text," *Journal of the American Academy of Religion* 49, no. 1 (March 1981): 35–49, https://www.jstor.org/stable/1462992.

9. Isaac Maddow-Zimet and Candace Gibson, "Despite Bans, Number of Abortions in the United States Increased in 2023," Guttmacher Institute, updated May 10, 2024, https://www.guttmacher.org/2024/03/despite-bans-number-abortions-united-states-increased-2023.

10. Derek Thompson, "The Americans Who Need Chaos," *Atlantic*, February 23, 2024, https://www.theatlantic.com/ideas/archive/2024/02/need-for-chaos-political-science-concept/677536.

11. Lydia Saad, "'Pro-Choice' Identification Rises to Near Record High in U.S.," Gallup, June 2, 2022, https://news.gallup.com/poll/393104/pro-choice-identification-rises-near-record-high.aspx.

12. Gabriel Borelli, "Americans Overwhelmingly Say Access to IVF Is a Good Thing," Pew Research Center, May 13, 2024, https://www.pewresearch.org/short-reads/2024/05/13/americans-overwhelmingly-say-access-to-ivf-is-a-good-thing.

13. Perry Bacon Jr., "I Left the Church—and Now Long for a 'Church for the Nones,'" *Washington Post*, August 21, 2023, https://www.washingtonpost.com/opinions/2023/08/21/leaving-christianity-religion-church-community.

14. Ross Douthat, "Where Should Agnostics Go on Sundays?," *New York Times*, September 1, 2023, https://www.nytimes.com/2023/09/01/opinion/church-nones.html.

15. Gordon W. Allport, *The Nature of Prejudice* (Addison-Wesley, 1954).

16. Nancy Gibbs, "Why? the Killing Fields of Rwanda," *TIME*, May 16, 1994, https://time.com/archive/6725331/why-the-killing-fields-of-rwanda.

17. William A. Donohue, "The Identity Trap: The Language of Genocide," *Journal of Language and Social Psychology* 31, no. 1 (March 2012): 13–29, https://doi.org/10.1177/0261927X11425033.

Epilogue

1. Maya Angelou, *All God's Children Need Traveling Shoes* (Random House, 1986), 196.

RYAN P. BURGE

(PhD, Southern Illinois University) is professor of practice at Washington University's Danforth Center on Religion and Politics. He is the author of *The Nones: Where They Came From, Who They Are, and Where They Are Going*; *Twenty Myths About Religion and Politics in America*; and *The American Religious Landscape: Facts, Trends, and the Future*. He served as lead researcher for *The Great Dechurching: Who's Leaving, Why Are They Going, and What Will It Take to Bring Them Back?* Until 2024 he was senior pastor of First Baptist Church of Mount Vernon, Illinois.

CONNECT WITH RYAN:

- @ryanburge
- ryanburgewrites
- graphsaboutreligion
- ryan.burge
- graphsaboutreligion